The Faber Book of
Contemporary Irish Poetry

The Faber Book of
CONTEMPORARY
IRISH POETRY

Edited by
Paul Muldoon

ff

faber and faber
LONDON · BOSTON

First published in 1986
by Faber and Faber Limited
3 Queen Square London WC1N 3AU

Filmset in Wilmaset Birkenhead Wirral
Printed in England by Clays Ltd, St Ives plc
All rights reserved

A CIP record for this book
is available from the British Library

ISBN 0-571-13761-X

Contents

[7]

LOUIS MACNEICE   1907–1963

CONTENTS

THOMAS KINSELLA   1928–

JOHN MONTAGUE   1929–

MICHAEL LONGLEY 1939–

SEAMUS HEANEY 1939–

CONTENTS

DEREK MAHON   1941–

PAUL DURCAN 1944–

TOM PAULIN 1949–

MEDBH McGUCKIAN 1950–

CONTENTS

Prologue

HIGGINS: When the BBC ask us to discuss modern poetry I assume they mean us to discuss the spirit informing poetry written in English since the European War; in other words, they expect us to consider the inner features most evident in the poetry of today. The abundance of such verse is, of course, written in England. I suppose you admit that?

MACNEICE: And America.

HIGGINS: I claim that pure poetry comes from Ireland.

MACNEICE: What do you mean by pure poetry?

HIGGINS: Well, pure poetry can only be gauged by standards. If one has a gold standard on which the quality of gold is assessed, one exercises a similar assessment on the standard of poetry, and that standard is based upon critical estimates in English literature, at least since Philip Sidney.

MACNEICE: This is an impure age, so it follows that much of its poetry, if it is honest – and poetry must be honest even before it is beautiful – must be impure.

HIGGINS: For me truth is still beauty, and beauty truth. As for the impurities, I can see the point, but I am not concerned with the impurities of modern English verse; I naturally prefer to discuss modern Irish poetry. Modern poetry, mark you, as distinct from modernist. Yeats was most modern without being modernist.

MACNEICE: So, in my opinion, is W. H. Auden.

HIGGINS: Present-day Irish poets are believers – heretical believers, maybe – but they have the spiritual buoyancy of a belief in something. The sort of belief I see in Ireland is a belief emanating from life, from nature, from revealed religion, and from the nation. A sort of dream that produces a sense of magic. Reading through the anthologies made from contemporary English poets I would say that there is little sign of such magic;

[17]

indeed there are few signs of the awful sense of respect for words which poetry demands.

MACNEICE: Perhaps half-a-dozen poems in fifty, which is not a bad average.

HIGGINS: I gladly concede half-a-dozen, but I will say that in general English verse speech is chaotic. Of course there may be magic in chaos. I am afraid, Mr MacNeice, you, as an Irishman, cannot escape from your blood, nor from our blood-music that brings the racial character to mind. Irish poetry remains a creation happily, fundamentally rooted in rural civilization, yet aware of and in touch with the elementals of the future. We have seen the drift of English poetry during the past few centuries – the retreat from the field to the park, from the pavement to the macadamed street, from the human zoological garden to the cinder heap where English verse so pathetically droops today.

MACNEICE: I have the feeling that you have sidetracked me into an Ireland versus England match. I am so little used to thinking of poetry in terms of race-consciousness that no doubt this was very good for me. However, I am still unconverted. I think one may have such a thing as one's racial blood-music, but that, like one's unconscious, it may be left to take care of itself. Compared with you, I take a rather common-sense view of poetry. I think that the poet is a sensitive instrument designed to record anything which interests his mind or affects his emotions. If a gasometer, for instance, affects his emotions, or if the Marxian dialectic, let us say, interests his mind, then let them come into his poetry. He will be fulfilling his function as a poet if he records these things with integrity and with as much music as he can compass or as is appropriate to the subject.

Drawn from *Tendencies in Modern Poetry*, a discussion between F. R. Higgins and Louis MacNeice, broadcast from Northern Ireland, and reprinted in the *Listener*, 27 July 1939.

PATRICK KAVANAGH   1904–1967

Inniskeen Road: July Evening

The bicycles go by in twos and threes –
There's a dance in Billy Brennan's barn tonight,
And there's the half-talk code of mysteries
And the wink-and-elbow language of delight.
Half-past eight and there is not a spot
Upon a mile of road, no shadow thrown
That might turn out a man or woman, not
A footfall tapping secrecies of stone.

I have what every poet hates in spite
Of all the solemn talk of contemplation.
Oh, Alexander Selkirk knew the plight
Of being king and government and nation.
A road, a mile of kingdom, I am king
Of banks and stones and every blooming thing.

To the Man after the Harrow

Now leave the check-reins slack,
The seed is flying far today –
The seed like stars against the black
Eternity of April clay.

This seed is potent as the seed
Of knowledge in the Hebrew Book,
So drive your horses in the creed
Of God the Father as a stook.

[21]

Forget the men on Brady's hill.
Forget what Brady's boy may say.
For destiny will not fulfil
Unless you let the harrow play.

Forget the worm's opinion too
Of hooves and pointed harrow-pins,
For you are driving your horses through
The mist where Genesis begins.

from Tarry Flynn

On an apple-ripe September morning
Through the mist-chill fields I went
With a pitch-fork on my shoulder
Less for use than for devilment.

The threshing mill was set-up, I knew,
In Cassidy's haggard last night,
And we owed them a day at the threshing
Since last year. O it was delight

To be paying bills of laughter
And chaffy gossip in kind
With work thrown in to ballast
The fantasy-soaring mind.

As I crossed the wooden bridge I wondered
As I looked into the drain
If ever a summer morning should find me
Shovelling up eels again.

And I thought of the wasps' nest in the bank
And how I got chased one day
Leaving the drag and the scraw-knife behind,
How I covered my face with hay.

The wet leaves of the cocksfoot
Polished my boots as I
Went round by the glistening bog-holes
Lost in unthinking joy.

I'll be carrying bags today, I mused,
The best job at the mill
With plenty of time to talk of our loves
As we wait for the bags to fill.

Maybe Mary might call round . . .
And then I came to the haggard gate,
And I knew as I entered that I had come
Through fields that were part of no earthly estate.

Shancoduff

My black hills have never seen the sun rising,
Eternally they look north towards Armagh.
Lot's wife would not be salt if she had been
Incurious as my black hills that are happy
When dawn whitens Glassdrummond chapel.

My hills hoard the bright shillings of March
While the sun searches in every pocket.
They are my Alps and I have climbed the Matterhorn
With a sheaf of hay for three perishing calves
In the field under the Big Forth of Rocksavage.

The sleety winds fondle the rushy beards of Shancoduff
While the cattle-drovers sheltering in the Featherna Bush
Look up and say: 'Who owns them hungry hills
That the water-hen and snipe must have forsaken?
A poet? Then by heavens he must be poor.'
I hear and is my heart not badly shaken?

Peace

And sometimes I am sorry when the grass
Is growing over the stones in quiet hollows
And the cocksfoot leans across the rutted cart-pass
That I am not the voice of country fellows
Who now are standing by some headland talking

Of turnips and potatoes or young corn
Or turf banks stripped for victory.
Here Peace is still hawking
His coloured combs and scarves and beads of horn.

Upon a headland by a whiny hedge
A hare sits looking down a leaf-lapped furrow,
There's an old plough upside-down on a weedy ridge
And someone is shouldering home a saddle-harrow.
Out of that childhood country what fools climb
To fight with tyrants Love and Life and Time?

Pursuit of an Ideal

November is come and I wait for you still
O nimble-footed nymph who slipped me when
I sighted you among some silly men
And charged you with the power of my will.
Headlong I charged to make a passionate kill,
Too easy, far too easy, I cried then,
You were not worth one drop from off my pen.
O flower of the common light, the thrill
Of common things raised up to angelhood
Leaped in your flirt-wild legs, I followed you
Through April May and June into September,
And still you kept your lead till passion's food
Went stale within my satchel. Now I woo
The footprints that you make across November.

The Great Hunger

I

Clay is the word and clay is the flesh
Where the potato-gatherers like mechanized scarecrows
                                                    move
Along the side-fall of the hill – Maguire and his men.
If we watch them an hour is there anything we can prove
Of life as it is broken-backed over the Book
Of Death? Here crows gabble over worms and frogs
And the gulls like old newspapers are blown clear of the
                                            hedges, luckily.
Is there some light of imagination in these wet clods?
Or why do we stand here shivering?
                                    Which of these men
Loved the light and the queen
Too long virgin? Yesterday was summer. Who was it
                        promised marriage to himself
Before apples were hung from the ceilings for Hallowe'en?
We will wait and watch the tragedy to the last curtain,
Till the last soul passively like a bag of wet clay
Rolls down the side of the hill, diverted by the angles
Where the plough missed or a spade stands, straitening
                                                the way.

A dog lying on a torn jacket under a heeled-up cart,
A horse nosing along the posied headland, trailing
A rusty plough. Three heads hanging between wide-apart
Legs. October playing a symphony on a slack wire paling.

[26]

Maguire watches the drills flattened out
And the flints that lit a-candle for him on a June altar
Flameless. The drills slipped by and the days slipped by
And he trembled his head away and ran free from the
                                                    world's halter,
And thought himself wiser than any man in the townland
When he laughed over pints of porter
Of how he came free from every net spread
In the gaps of experience. He shook a knowing head
And pretended to his soul
That children are tedious in hurrying fields of April
Where men are spanging across wide furrows.
Lost in the passion that never needs a wife –
The pricks that pricked were the pointed pins of harrows.
Children scream so loud that the crows could bring
The seed of an acre away with crow-rude jeers.
Patrick Maguire, he called his dog and he flung a stone in
                                                    the air
And hallooed the birds away that were the birds of the
                                                    years.

Turn over the weedy clods and tease out the tangled skeins.
What is he looking for there?
He thinks it is a potato, but we know better
Than his mud-gloved fingers probe in this insensitive hair.

'Move forward the basket and balance it steady
In this hollow. Pull down the shafts of that cart, Joe,
And straddle the horse,' Maguire calls.
'The wind's over Brannagan's, now that means rain.
Graip up some withered stalks and see that no potato falls
Over the tail-board going down the ruckety pass –

And *that's* a job we'll have to do in December,
Gravel it and build a kerb on the bog-side. Is that Cassidy's
                                                              ass
Out in my clover? Curse o' God –
Where is that dog?
Never where he's wanted.' Maguire grunts and spits
Through a clay-wattled moustache and stares about him
                                                from the height.
His dream changes again like the cloud-swung wind
And he is not so sure now if his mother was right
When she praised the man who made a field his bride.

Watch him, watch him, that man on a hill whose spirit
Is a wet sack flapping about the knees of time.
He lives that his little fields may stay fertile when his own
                                                              body
Is spread in the bottom of a ditch under two coulters
                                      crossed in Christ's Name.

He was suspicious in his youth as a rat near strange bread,
When girls laughed; when they screamed he knew that
                                                            meant
The cry of fillies in season. He could not walk
The easy road to destiny. He dreamt
The innocence of young brambles to hooked treachery.
O the grip, O the grip of irregular fields! No man escapes.
It could not be that back of the hills love was free
And ditches straight.
No monster hand lifted up children and put down apes
As here.
                              'O God if I had been wiser!'

That was his sigh like the brown breeze in the thistles.
He looks towards his house and haggard. 'O God if I had
                                 been wiser!'
But now a crumpled leaf from the whitethorn bushes
Darts like a frightened robin, and the fence
Shows the green of after-grass through a little window,
And he knows that his own heart is calling his mother a liar
God's truth is life – even the grotesque shapes of its foulest
                                     fire.

The horse lifts its head and cranes
Through the whins and stones
To lip late passion in the crawling clover.
In the gap there's a bush weighted with boulders like
                                 morality,
The fools of life bleed if they climb over.

The wind leans from Brady's, and the coltsfoot leaves are
                             holed with rust,
Rain fills the cart-tracks and the sole-plate grooves;
A yellow sun reflects in Donaghmoyne
The poignant light in puddles shaped by hooves.

Come with me, Imagination, into this iron house
And we will watch from the doorway the years run back,
And we will know what a peasant's left hand wrote on the
                                     page.
Be easy, October. No cackle hen, horse neigh, tree sough,
                                  duck quack.

II

Maguire was faithful to death:
He stayed with his mother till she died
At the age of ninety-one.
She stayed too long,
Wife and mother in one.
When she died
The knuckle-bones were cutting the skin of her son's
                                                    backside

And he was sixty-five.

O he loved his mother
Above all others.
O he loved his ploughs
And he loved his cows
And his happiest dream
Was to clean his arse
With perennial grass
On the bank of some summer stream;
To smoke his pipe
In a sheltered gripe
In the middle of July –
His face in a mist
And two stones in his fist
And an impotent worm on his thigh.

But his passion became a plague
For he grew feeble bringing the vague
Women of his mind to lust nearness,
Once a week at least flesh must make an appearance.

So Maguire got tired
Of the no-target gun fired
And returned to his headland of carrots and cabbage
To the fields once again
Where eunuchs can be men
And life is more lousy than savage.

III

Poor Paddy Maguire, a fourteen-hour day
He worked for years. It was he that lit the fire
And boiled the kettle and gave the cows their hay.
His mother tall hard as a Protestant spire
Came down the stairs barefoot at the kettle-call
And talked to her son sharply: 'Did you let
The hens out, you?' She had a venomous drawl
And a wizened face like moth-eaten leatherette.
Two black cats peeped between the banisters
And gloated over the bacon-fizzling pan.
Outside the window showed tin canisters.
The snipe of Dawn fell like a whirring stone
And Patrick on a headland stood alone.

The pull is on the traces, it is March
And a cold black wind is blowing from Dundalk.
The twisting sod rolls over on her back –
The virgin screams before the irresistible sock.
No worry on Maguire's mind this day
Except that he forgot to bring his matches.
'Hop back there Polly, hoy back, woa, wae,'
From every second hill a neighbour watches
With all the sharpened interest of rivalry.

Yet sometimes when the sun comes through a gap
These men know God the Father in a tree:
The Holy Spirit is the rising sap,
And Christ will be the green leaves that will come
At Easter from the sealed and guarded tomb.

Primroses and the unearthly start of ferns
Among the blackthorn shadows in the ditch,
A dead sparrow and an old waistcoat. Maguire learns
As the horses turn slowly round the which is which
Of love and fear and things half born to mind.
He stands between the plough-handles and he sees
At the end of a long furrow his name signed
Among the poets, prostitutes. With all miseries
He is one. Here with the unfortunate
Who for half-moments of paradise
Pay out good days and wait and wait
For sunlight-woven cloaks. O to be wise
As Respectability that knows the price of all things
And marks God's truth in pounds and pence and farthings.

IV

April, and no one able to calculate
How far is it to harvest. They put down
The seeds blindly with sensuous groping fingers,
And sensual sleep dreams subtly underground.
Tomorrow is Wednesday – who cares?
'Remember Eileen Farrelly? I was thinking
A man might do a damned sight worse . . .' That voice is
                                                    blown

Through a hole in a garden wall –
And who was Eileen now cannot be known.

The cattle are out on grass,
The corn is coming up evenly.
The farm folk are hurrying to catch Mass:
Christ will meet them at the end of the world, the slow and
                                        speedier.
But the fields say: only Time can bless.

Maguire knelt beside a pillar where he could spit
Without being seen. He turned an old prayer round:
'Jesus, Mary and Joseph pray for us
Now and at the Hour.' Heaven dazzled death.
'Wonder should I cross-plough that turnip-ground.'
The tension broke. The congregation lifted its head
As one man and coughed in unison.
Five hundred hearts were hungry for life –
Who lives in Christ shall never die the death.
And the candle-lit Altar and the flowers
And the pregnant Tabernacle lifted a moment to Prophecy
Out of the clayey hours.
Maguire sprinkled his face with holy water
As the congregation stood up for the Last Gospel.
He rubbed the dust off his knees with his palm, and then
Coughed the prayer phlegm up from his throat and
                                        sighed: Amen.

Once one day in June when he was walking
Among his cattle in the Yellow Meadow
He met a girl carrying a basket –
And he was then a young and heated fellow.
Too earnest, too earnest! He rushed beyond the thing
To the unreal. And he saw Sin
Written in letters larger than John Bunyan dreamt of.

[33]

For the strangled impulse there is no redemption.
And that girl was gone and he was counting
The dangers in the fields where love ranted
He was helpless. He saw his cattle
And stroked their flanks in lieu of wife to handle.
He would have changed the circle if he could,
The circle that was the grass track where he ran.
Twenty times a day he ran round the field
And still there was no winning-post where the runner is
                                         cheered home.

Desperately he broke the tune,
But however he tried always the same melody crept up
                                         from the background,
The dragging step of a ploughman going home through
                                         the guttery
Headlands under an April-watery moon.
Religion, the fields and the fear of the Lord
And Ignorance giving him the coward's blow,
He dare not rise to pluck the fantasies
From the fruited Tree of Life. He bowed his head
And saw a wet weed twined about his toe.

V

Evening at the cross-roads –
Heavy heads nodding out words as wise
As the rumination of cows after milking.
From the ragged road surface a boy picks up
A piece of gravel and stares at it – and then
He flings it across the elm tree on to the railway.
It means nothing,
Not a damn thing.

Somebody is coming over the metal railway bridge
And his hobnailed boots on the arches sound like a gong
Calling men awake. But the bridge is too narrow –
The men lift their heads a moment. That was only John,
So they dream on.

Night in the elms, night in the grass.
O we are too tired to go home yet. Two cyclists pass
Talking loudly of Kitty and Molly –
Horses or women? wisdom or folly?
A door closes on an evicted dog
Where prayers begin in Barney Meegan's kitchen;
Rosie curses the cat between her devotions;
The daughter prays that she may have three wishes –
Health and wealth and love –
From the fairy who is faith or hope or compounds of.

At the cross-roads the crowd had thinned out:
Last words are uttered. There is no tomorrow;
No future but only time stretched for the mowing of the hay
Or putting an axle in the turf-barrow.

Patrick Maguire went home and made cocoa
And broke a chunk off the loaf of wheaten bread;
His mother called down to him to look again
And make sure that the hen-house was locked. His sister
                                        grunted in bed.
The sound of a sow taking up a new position.
Pat opened his trousers wide over the ashes
And dreamt himself to lewd sleepiness.
The clock ticked on. Time passes.

VI

Health and wealth and love he too dreamt of in May
As he sat on the railway slope and watched the children of
the place
Picking up a primrose here and a daisy there –
They were picking up life's truth singly. But he dreamt of
the Absolute envased bouquet –
All or nothing. And it was nothing. For God is not all
In one place, complete
Till Hope comes in and takes it on his shoulder –
O Christ, that is what you have done for us:
In a crumb of bread the whole mystery is.

He read the symbol too sharply and turned
From the five simple doors of sense
To the door whose combination lock has puzzled
Philosopher and priest and common dunce.

Men build their heavens as they build their circles
Of friends. God is in the bits and pieces of Everyday –
A kiss here and a laugh again, and sometimes tears,
A pearl necklace round the neck of poverty.

He sat on the railway slope and watched the evening,
Too beautifully perfect to use,
And his three wishes were three stones too sharp to sit on,
Too hard to carve. Three frozen idols of a speechless muse.

VII

'Now go to Mass and pray and confess your sins
And you'll have all the luck,' his mother said.

He listened to the lie that is a woman's screen
Around a conscience when soft thighs are spread.
And all the while she was setting up the lie
She trusted in Nature that never deceives.
But her son took it as literal truth.
Religion's walls expand to the push of nature. Morality
                                                    yields
To sense – but not in little tillage fields.

Life went on like that. One summer morning
Again through a hay-field on her way to the shop –
The grass was wet and over-leaned the path –
And Agnes held her skirts sensationally up,
And not because the grass was wet either.
A man was watching her, Patrick Maguire.
She was in love with passion and its weakness
And the wet grass could never cool the fire
That radiated from her unwanted womb
In that country, in that metaphysical land
Where flesh was a thought more spiritual than music
Among the stars – out of reach of the peasant's hand.

Ah, but the priest was one of the people too –
A farmer's son – and surely he knew
The needs of a brother and sister.
Religion could not be a counter-irritant like a blister,
But the certain standard measured and known
By which man might re-make his soul though all walls
                                                    were down
And all earth's pedestalled gods thrown.

VIII

Sitting on a wooden gate,
Sitting on a wooden gate,
Sitting on a wooden gate
He didn't care a damn.
Said whatever came into his head,
Said whatever came into his head,
Said whatever came into his head
And inconsequently sang.
While his world withered away,
He had a cigarette to smoke and a pound to spend
On drink the next Saturday.
His cattle were fat
And his horses all that
Midsummer grass could make them.

The young women ran wild
And dreamed of a child
Joy dreams though the fathers might forsake them
But no one would take them,
No one would take them;
No man could ever see
That their skirts had loosed buttons,
O the men were as blind as could be.
And Patrick Maguire
From his purgatory fire
Called the gods of the Christian to prove
That this twisted skein
Was the necessary pain
And not the rope that was strangling true love.

But sitting on a wooden gate
Sometime in July
When he was thirty-four or five
He gloried in the lie:
He made it read the way it should,
He made life read the evil good
While he cursed the ascetic brotherhood
Without knowing why.
Sitting on a wooden gate
All, all alone
He sang and laughed
Like a man quite daft,
Or like a man on a channel raft
He fantasied forth his groan.
Sitting on a wooden gate,
Sitting on a wooden gate,
Sitting on a wooden gate
He rode in day-dream cars.
He locked his body with his knees
When the gate swung too much in the breeze.
But while he caught high ecstasies
Life slipped between the bars.

IX

He gave himself another year,
Something was bound to happen before then –
The circle would break down
And he would curve the new one to his own will.

A new rhythm is a new life
And in it marriage is hung and money.
He would be a new man walking through unbroken
                                              meadows
Of dawn in the year of One.

The poor peasant talking to himself in a stable door –
An ignorant peasant deep in dung.
What can the passers-by think otherwise?
Where is his silver bowl of knowledge hung?
Why should men be asked to believe in a soul
That is only the mark of a hoof in guttery gaps?
A man is what is written on the label.
And the passing world stares but no one stops
To look closer. So back to the growing crops
And the ridges he never loved.
Nobody will ever know how much tortured poetry the
                              pulled weeds on the ridge wrote
Before they withered in the July sun,
Nobody will ever read the wild, sprawling, scrawling mad
                                        woman's signature,
The hysteria and the boredom of the enclosed nun of his
                                                thought.
Like the afterbirth of a cow stretched on a branch in the
                                                wind
Life dried in the veins of these women and men:
The grey and grief and unlove,
The bones in the backs of their hands,
And the chapel pressing its low ceiling over them.

Sometimes they did laugh and see the sunlight,
A narrow slice of divine instruction.
Going along the river at the bend of Sunday
The trout played in the pools encouragement
To jump in love though death bait the hook.
And there would be girls sitting on the grass banks of
lanes.

Stretch-legged and lingering staring –
A man might take one of them if he had the courage.
But 'No' was in every sentence of their story
Except when the public-house came in and shouted its
piece.

The yellow buttercups and the bluebells among the whin
bushes
On rocks in the middle of ploughing
Was a bright spoke in the wheel
Of the peasant's mill.
The goldfinches on the railway paling were worth looking
at –

A man might imagine then
Himself in Brazil and these birds the birds of paradise
And the Amazon and the romance traced on the school
map lived again.

Talk in evening corners and under trees
Was like an old book found in a king's tomb.
The children gathered round like students and listened
And some of the saga defied the draught in the open tomb
And was not blown.

X

Their intellectual life consisted in reading
Reynolds News or the *Sunday Dispatch*,
With sometimes an old almanac brought down from the
ceiling
Or a school reader brown with the droppings of thatch.
The sporting results or the headlines of war
Was a humbug profound as the highbrow's Arcana.
Pat tried to be wise to the abstraction of all that
But its secret dribbled down his waistcoat like a drink from
a strainer.

He wagered a bob each way on the Derby,
He got a straight tip from a man in a shop –
A double from the Guineas it was and thought himself
A master mathematician when one of them came up
And he could explain how much he'd have drawn
On the double if the second leg had followed the first.
He was betting on form and breeding, he claimed,
And the man that did that could never be burst.
After that they went on to the war, and the generals
On both sides were shown to be stupid as hell.
If he'd taken *that* road, they remarked of a Marshal,
He'd have . . . O they know their geography well.
This was their university. Maguire was an undergraduate
Who dreamed from his lowly position of rising
To a professorship like Larry McKenna or Duffy
Or the pig-gelder Nallon whose knowledge was amazing.
'A treble, full multiple odds . . . That's flat porter . . .
My turnips are destroyed with the blackguardly crows . . .

Another one . . . No, you're wrong about that thing I was
                                         telling you . . .
Did you part with your filly, Jack? I heard that you sold
                                         her . . .'
The students were all savants by the time of pub-close.

XI

A year passed and another hurried after it
And Patrick Maguire was still six months behind life –
His mother six months ahead of it;
His sister straddle-legged across it –
One leg in hell and the other in heaven
And between the purgatory of middle-aged virginity –
She prayed for release to heaven or hell.
His mother's voice grew thinner like a rust-worn knife
But it cut venomously as it thinned,
It cut him up the middle till he became more woman than
                                         man,
And it cut through to his mind before the end.

Another field whitened in the April air
And the harrows rattled over the seed.
He gathered the loose stones off the ridges carefully
And grumbled to his men to hurry. He looked like a man
                          who could give advice
To foolish young fellows. He was forty-seven,
And there was depth in his jaw and his voice was the voice
                          of a great cattle-dealer,
A man with whom the fair-green gods break even.

[43]

'I think I ploughed that lea the proper depth,
She ought to give a crop if any land gives . . .
Drive slower with the foal-mare, Joe.'
Joe, a young man of imagined wives,
Smiled to himself and answered like a slave:
'You needn't fear or fret.
I'm taking her as easy, as easy as . . .
Easy there Fanny, easy, pet.'

They loaded the day-scoured implements on the cart
As the shadows of poplars crookened the furrows.
It was the evening, evening. Patrick was forgetting to be
                                                    lonely
As he used to be in Aprils long ago.
It was the menopause, the misery-pause.

The schoolgirls passed his house laughing every morning
And sometimes they spoke to him familiarly –
He had an idea. Schoolgirls of thirteen
Would see no political intrigue in an old man's friendship.
Love
The heifer waiting to be nosed by the old bull.

The notion passed too – there was the danger of talk
And jails are narrower than the five-sod ridge
And colder than the black hills facing Armagh in February.
He sinned over the warm ashes again and his crime
The law's long arm could not serve with 'time'.

His face set like an old judge's pose:
Respectability and righteousness,
Stand for no nonsense.
The priest from the altar called Patrick Maguire's name
To hold the collecting-box in the chapel door
During all the Sundays of May.
His neighbours envied him his holy rise,
But he walked down from the church with affected
          indifference
And took the measure of heaven angle-wise.

He still could laugh and sing,
But not the wild laugh or the abandoned harmony now
That called the world to new silliness from the top of a
          wooden gate
When thirty-five could take the sparrow's bow.
Let us be kind, let us be kind and sympathetic:
Maybe life is not for joking or for finding happiness in –
This tiny light in Oriental Darkness
Looking out chance windows of poetry or prayer.

And the grief and defeat of men like these peasants
Is God's way – maybe – and we must not want too much
To see.
The twisted thread is stronger than the wind-swept fleece.
And in the end who shall rest in truth's high peace?
Or whose is the world now, even now?
O let us kneel where the blind ploughman kneels
And learn to live without despairing
In a mud-walled space –
Illiterate, unknown and unknowing.
Let us kneel where he kneels
And feel what he feels.

One day he saw a daisy and he thought it
Reminded him of his childhood –
He stopped his cart to look at it.
Was there a fairy hiding behind it?

He helped a poor woman whose cow
Had died on her;
He dragged home a drunken man on a winter's night;
And one rare moment he heard the young people playing
                              on the railway stile
And he wished them happiness and whatever they most
                              desired from life.

He saw the sunlight and begrudged no man
His share of what the miserly soil and soul
Gives in a season to a ploughman.
And he cried for his own loss one late night on the pillow
And yet thanked the God who had arranged these things.

Was he then a saint?
A Matt Talbot of Monaghan?

His sister Mary Anne spat poison at the children
Who sometimes came to the door selling raffle tickets
For holy funds.
'Get out, you little tramps!' she would scream
As she shook to the hens an armful of crumbs,
But Patrick often put his hand deep down
In his trouser-pocket and fingered out a penny
Or maybe a tobacco-stained caramel.
'You're soft,' said the sister; 'with other people's money
It's not a bit funny.'

The cards are shuffled and the deck
Laid flat for cutting – Tom Malone
Cut for trump. I think we'll make
This game, the last, a tanner one.
Hearts. Right. I see you're breaking
Your two-year-old. Play quick, Maguire,
The clock there says it half-past ten –
Kate, throw another sod on that fire.
One of the card-players laughs and spits
Into the flame across a shoulder.
Outside, a noise like a rat
Among the hen-roosts. The cock crows over
The frosted townland of the night.
Eleven o'clock and still the game
Goes on and the players seem to be
Drunk in an Orient opium den.
Midnight, one o'clock, two.
Somebody's leg has fallen asleep.
What about home? Maguire, are you
Using your double-tree this week?
Why? do you want it? Play the ace.
There's it, and that's the last card for me.
A wonderful night, we had. Duffy's place
Is very convenient. Is that a ghost or a tree?
And so they go home with dragging feet
And their voices rumble like laden carts.
And they are happy as the dead or sleeping . . .
I should have led that ace of hearts.

XII

The fields were bleached white,
The wooden tubs full of water
Were white in the winds
That blew through Brannagan's Gap on their way from
Siberia;
The cows on the grassless heights
Followed the hay that had wings –
The February fodder that hung itself on the black branches
Of the hill-top hedge.
A man stood beside a potato-pit
And clapped his arms
And pranced on the crisp roots
And shouted to warm himself.
Then he buck-leaped about the potatoes
And scooped them into a basket.
He looked like a bucking suck-calf
Whose spine was being tickled.
Sometimes he stared across the bogs
And sometimes he straightened his back and vaguely
whistled
A tune that weakened his spirit
And saddened his terrier dog's.
A neighbour passed with a spade on his shoulder
And Patrick Maguire bent like a bridge
Whistled – good morning under his oxter,
And the man the other side of the hedge
Champed his spade on the road at his toes
And talked an old sentimentality
While the wind blew under his clothes.

The mother sickened and stayed in bed all day,
Her head hardly dented the pillow, so light and thin it had
                                                                   worn,
But she still enquired after the household affairs.
She held the strings of her children's Punch and Judy, and
                                                    when a mouth opened
It was her truth that the dolls would have spoken
If they hadn't been made of wood and tin –
'Did you open the barn door, Pat, to let the young calves in?'
The priest called to see her every Saturday
And she told him her troubles and fears:
'If Mary Anne was settled I'd die in peace –
I'm getting on in years.'
'You were a good woman,' said the priest,
'And your children will miss you when you're gone.
The likes of you this parish never knew,
I'm sure they'll not forget the work you've done.'
She reached five bony crooks under the tick –
'Five pounds for Masses – won't you say them quick.'
She died one morning in the beginning of May
And a shower of sparrow-notes was the litany for her dying.
The holy water was sprinkled on the bed-clothes
And her children stood around the bed and cried because it
                                                    was too late for crying.
A mother dead! The tired sentiment:
'Mother, Mother' was a shallow pool
Where sorrow hardly could wash its feet . . .
Mary Anne came away from the deathbed and boiled the
                                                    calves their gruel.
O what was I doing when the procession passed?
Where was I looking?

Young women and men
And I might have joined them.
Who bent the coin of my destiny
That it stuck in the slot?
I remember a night we walked
Through the moon of Donaghmoyne,
Four of us seeking adventure,
It was midsummer forty years ago.
Now I know
The moment that gave the turn to my life.
O Christ! I am locked in a stable with pigs and cows for ever.

XIII

The world looks on
And talks of the peasant:
The peasant has no worries;
In his little lyrical fields
He ploughs and sows;
He eats fresh food,
He loves fresh women,
He is his own master
As it was in the Beginning
The simpleness of peasant life.
The birds that sing for him are eternal choirs,
Everywhere he walks there are flowers.
His heart is pure,
His mind is clear,
He can talk to God as Moses and Isaiah talked –
The peasant who is only one remove from the beasts he drives.
The travellers stop their cars to gape over the green bank
                                                    into his fields –

There is the source from which all cultures rise,
And all religions,
There is the pool in which the poet dips
And the musician.
Without the peasant base civilization must die,
Unless the clay is in the mouth the singer's singing is useless.
The travellers touch the roots of the grass and feel renewed
When they grasp the steering wheels again.
The peasant is the unspoiled child of Prophecy,
The peasant is all virtues – let us salute him without irony
The peasant ploughman who is half a vegetable –
Who can react to sun and rain and sometimes even
Regret that the Maker of Light had not touched him more
                                            intensely.
Brought him up from the sub-soil to an existence
Of conscious joy. He was not born blind.
He is not always blind: sometimes the cataract yields
To sudden stone-falling or the desire to breed.

The girls pass along the roads
And he can remember what man is,
But there is nothing he can do.
Is there nothing he can do?
Is there no escape?
No escape, no escape.

The cows and horses breed,
And the potato-seed
Gives a bud and a root and rots
In the good mother's way with her sons;
The fledged bird is thrown
From the nest – on its own.

[51]

But the peasant in his little acres is tied
To a mother's womb by the wind-toughened navel-cord
Like a goat tethered to the stump of a tree –
He circles around and around wondering why it should be.
No crash,
No drama.
That was how his life happened.
No mad hooves galloping in the sky,
But the weak, washy way of true tragedy –
A sick horse nosing around the meadow for a clean place to
                                                              die.

XIV

We may come out into the October reality, Imagination,
The sleety wind no longer slants to the black hill where
                                                        Maguire
And his men are now collecting the scattered harness and
                                                        baskets.
The dog sitting on a wisp of dry stalks
Watches them through the shadows.
'Back in, back in.' One talks to the horse as to a brother.
Maguire himself is patting a potato-pit against the
                                                      weather –
An old man fondling a new-piled grave:
'Joe, I hope you didn't forget to hide the spade,
For there's rogues in the townland. Hide it flat in a furrow.
I think we ought to be finished by tomorrow.'
Their voices through the darkness sound like voices from a
                                                          cave,
A dull thudding far away, futile, feeble, far away,
First cousins to the ghosts of the townland.

[52]

A light stands in a window. Mary Anne
Has the table set and the tea-pot waiting in the ashes.
She goes to the door and listens and then she calls
From the top of the haggard-wall:
'What's keeping you
And the cows to be milked and all the other work there's to
do?'

'All right, all right,
We'll not stay here all night.'

Applause, applause,
The curtain falls.
Applause, applause
From the homing carts and the trees
And the bawling cows at the gates.
From the screeching water-hens
And the mill-race heavy with the Lammas floods curving
over the weir.
A train at the station blowing off steam
And the hysterical laughter of the defeated everywhere.
Night, and the futile cards are shuffled again.
Maguire spreads his legs over the impotent cinders that
wake no manhood now
And he hardly looks to see which card is trump.
His sister tightens her legs and her lips and frizzles up
Like the wick of an oil-less lamp.
The curtain falls –
Applause, applause.

Maguire is not afraid of death, the Church will light him a
                                                           candle
To see his way through the vaults and he'll understand the
Quality of the clay that dribbles over his coffin.
He'll know the names of the roots that climb down to tickle
                                                       his feet.
And he will feel no different than when he walked through
                                                  Donaghmoyne.
If he stretches out a hand – a wet clod,
If he opens his nostrils – a dungy smell;
If he opens his eyes once in a million years –
Through a crack in the crust of the earth he may see a face
                                                      nodding in
Or a woman's legs. Shut them again for that sight is sin.

He will hardly remember that life happened to him –
Something was brighter a moment. Somebody sang in the
                                                       distance.
A procession passed down a mesmerized street.
He remembers names like Easter and Christmas
By the colour his fields were.
Maybe he will be born again, a bird of an angel's conceit
To sing the gospel of life
To a music as flightily tangent
As a tune on an oboe.
And the serious look of the fields will have changed to the
                                                   leer of a hobo
Swaggering celestially home to his three wishes granted.
Will that be? will that be?
Or is the earth right that laughs haw-haw
And does not believe
In an unearthly law.

The earth that says:
Patrick Maguire, the old peasant, can neither be damned
                                     nor glorified:
The graveyard in which he will lie will be just a deep-
                                   drilled potato-field
Where the seed gets no chance to come through
To the fun of the sun.
The tongue in his mouth is the root of a yew.
Silence, silence. The story is done.

He stands in the doorway of his house
A ragged sculpture of the wind,
October creaks the rotted mattress
The bedposts fall. No hope. No lust.
The hungry fiend
Screams the apocalypse of clay
In every corner of this land.

Pegasus

My soul was an old horse
Offered for sale in twenty fairs.
I offered him to the Church – the buyers
Were little men who feared his unusual airs.
One said: 'Let him remain unbid
In the wind and rain and hunger
Of sin and we will get him –
With the winkers thrown in – for nothing.'

Then the men of State looked at
What I'd brought for sale.
One minister, wondering if
Another horse-body would fit the tail
That he'd kept for sentiment –
The relic of his own soul –
Said, 'I will graze him in lieu of his labour.'
I lent him for a week or more
And he came back a hurdle of bones,
Starved, overworked, in despair.
I nursed him on the roadside grass
To shape him for another fair.

I lowered my price. I stood him where
The broken-winded, spavined stand
And crooked shopkeepers said that he
Might do a season on the land –
But not for high-paid work in towns.
He'd do a tinker, possibly.
I begged, 'O make some offer now,
A soul is a poor man's tragedy.
He'll draw your dungiest cart,' I said,
'Show you short cuts to Mass,
Teach weather lore, at night collect
Bad debts from poor men's grass.'
                                    And they would not.

            Where the
Tinkers quarrel I went down
With my horse, my soul.
I cried, 'Who will bid me half a crown?'
From their rowdy bargaining

Not one turned. 'Soul,' I prayed,
'I have hawked you through the world
Of Church and State and meanest trade.
But this evening, halter off,
Never again will it go on.
On the south side of ditches
There is grazing of the sun.
No more haggling with the world . . .'

As I said these words he grew
Wings upon his back. Now I may ride him
Every land my imagination knew.

Temptation in Harvest

A poplar leaf was spiked upon a thorn
Above the hedge like a flag of surrender
That the year hung out. I was afraid to wonder
At capitulation in a field of corn.
The yellow posies in the headland grass
Paraded up and down in loud apparel;
If I could search their hearts I'd find a moral
For men and women – but I'd let them pass.
Hope guarantees the poor that they will be
Masters at haw-time when the robins are
Courageous as a crow or water-hen. O see
There someone on an ash tree's limb
Sawing a stick for a post or a drilling-bar!
I wish that I this moment were with him!

[57]

I should not have wished, should not have seen how white
The wings of thistle seeds are, and how gay
Amoral Autumn gives her soul away
And every maidenhead without a fight.
I turned to the stubble of the oats,
Knowing that clay could still seduce my heart
After five years of pavements raised to art.
O the devilry of the fields! petals that goats
Have plucked from rose bushes of vanity!
But here! a small blue flower creeping over
On a trailing stem across an inch-wide chasm.
Even here wild gods have set a net for sanity.
Where can I look and not become a lover
Terrified at each recurring spasm?

This time of the year mind worried
About the threshing of the corn and whether
The yellow streaks in the sunset were for fine weather.
The sides of the ricks were letting in; too hurried
We built them to beat the showers that were flying
All day. 'It's raining in Drummeril now,'
We'd speculate, half happy to think how
Flat on the ground a neighbour's stooks were lying.
Each evening combing the ricks like a lover's hair,
Gently combing the butt-ends to run the rain,
Then running to the gate to see if there
Was anybody travelling on the train.
The Man in the Moon has water on the brain!
I love one! but my ricks are more my care.

An old woman whispered from a bush: 'Stand in
The shadow of the ricks until she passes;
You cannot eat what grows upon Parnassus –
And she is going there as sure as sin.'
I saw her turn her head as she went down
The blackberry lane-way, and I knew
In my heart that only what we love is true –
And not what loves us, we should make our own.
I stayed in indecision by the gate,
As Christ in Gethsemane, to guess
Into the morrow and the day after,
And tried to keep from thinking on the fate
Of those whom beauty tickles into laughter
And leaves them on their backs in muddiness.

The air was drugged with Egypt. Could I go
Over the field to the City of the Kings
Where art, music, letters are the real things?
The stones of the street, the sheds, hedges cried, No.
Earth, earth! I dragged my feet off the ground.
Labourers, animals armed with farm tools,
Ringed me. The one open gap had larch poles
Across it now by memory secured and bound.
The flaggers in the swamp were the reserves
Waiting to lift their dim nostalgic arms
The moment I would move. The noise of carts
Softening into haggards wove new charms.
The simplest memory plays upon the nerves
Symphonies that break down what the will asserts.

O Life, forgive me for my sins! I can hear
In the elm by the potato-pits a thrush;
Rain is falling on the Burning Bush
Where God appeared. Why now do I fear
That clear in the sky where the Evening Star is born?
Why does the inconsequential gabble
Of an old man among the hills so trouble
My thoughts this September evening? Now I turn
Away from the ricks, the sheds, the cabbage garden,
The stones of the street, the thrush song in the tree,
The potato-pits, the flaggers in the swamp;
From the country heart that hardly learned to harden,
From the spotlight of an old-fashioned kitchen lamp
I go to follow her who winked at me.

Bluebells for Love

There will be bluebells growing under the big trees
And you will be there and I will be there in May;
For some other reason we both will have to delay
The evening in Dunshaughlin – to please
Some imagined relation,
So both of us came to walk through that plantation.

We will be interested in the grass,
In an old bucket-hoop, in the ivy that weaves
Green incongruity among dead leaves,
We will put on surprise at carts that pass –
Only sometimes looking sideways at the bluebells in the
plantation
And never frighten them with too wild an exclamation.

We will be wise, we will not let them guess
That we are watching them or they will pose
A mere façade like boys
Caught out in virtue's naturalness.
We will not impose on the bluebells in that plantation
Too much of our desire's adulation.

We will have other loves – or so they'll think;
The primroses or the ferns or the briars,
Or even the rusty paling wires,
Or the violets on the sunless sorrel bank.
Only as an aside the bluebells in the plantation
Will mean a thing to our dark contemplation.

We'll know love little by little, glance by glance.
Ah, the clay under these roots is so brown!
We'll steal from Heaven while God is in the town –
I caught an angel smiling in a chance
Look through the tree-trunks of the plantation
As you and I walked slowly to the station.

Advent

We have tested and tasted too much, lover –
Through a chink too wide there comes in no wonder.
But here in the Advent-darkened room
Where the dry black bread and the sugarless tea
Of penance will charm back the luxury
Of a child's soul, we'll return to Doom
The knowledge we stole but could not use.

And the newness that was in every stale thing
When we looked at it as children: the spirit-shocking
Wonder in a black slanting Ulster hill
Or the prophetic astonishment in the tedious talking
Of an old fool will awake for us and bring
You and me to the yard gate to watch the whins
And the bog-holes, cart-tracks, old stables where Time begins.

O after Christmas we'll have no need to go searching
For the difference that sets an old phrase burning –
We'll hear it in the whispered argument of a churning
Or in the streets where the village boys are lurching.
And we'll hear it among decent men too
Who barrow dung in gardens under trees,
Wherever life pours ordinary plenty.
Won't we be rich, my love and I, and please
God we shall not ask for reason's payment,
The why of heart-breaking strangeness in dreeping hedges
Nor analyse God's breath in common statement.
We have thrown into the dust-bin the clay-minted wages
Of pleasure, knowledge and the conscious hour –
And Christ comes with a January flower.

A Christmas Childhood

I

One side of the potato-pits was white with frost –
How wonderful that was, how wonderful!
And when we put our ears to the paling-post
The music that came out was magical.

The light between the ricks of hay and straw
Was a hole in Heaven's gable. An apple tree
With its December-glinting fruit we saw –
O you, Eve, were the world that tempted me

To eat the knowledge that grew in clay
And death the germ within it! Now and then
I can remember something of the gay
Garden that was childhood's. Again

The tracks of cattle to a drinking-place,
A green stone lying sideways in a ditch
Or any common sight the transfigured face
Of a beauty that the world did not touch.

II

My father played the melodeon
Outside at our gate;
There were stars in the morning east
And they danced to his music.

Across the wild bogs his melodeon called
To Lennons and Callans.
As I pulled on my trousers in a hurry
I knew some strange thing had happened.

Outside in the cow-house my mother
Made the music of milking;
The light of her stable-lamp was a star
And the frost of Bethlehem made it twinkle.

A water-hen screeched in the bog,
Mass-going feet
Crunched the wafer-ice on the pot-holes,
Somebody wistfully twisted the bellows wheel.

My child poet picked out the letters
On the grey stone,
In silver the wonder of a Christmas townland,
The winking glitter of a frosty dawn.

Cassiopeia was over
Cassidy's hanging hill,
I looked and three whin bushes rode across
The horizon – the Three Wise Kings.

An old man passing said:
'Can't he make it talk' –
The melodeon. I hid in the doorway
And tightened the belt of my box-pleated coat.

I nicked six nicks on the door-post
With my penknife's big blade –
There was a little one for cutting tobacco.
And I was six Christmases of age.

My father played the melodeon,
My mother milked the cows,
And I had a prayer like a white rose pinned
On the Virgin Mary's blouse.

Memory of my Father

Every old man I see
Reminds me of my father
When he had fallen in love with death
One time when sheaves were gathered.

That man I saw in Gardner Street
Stumble on the kerb was one,
He stared at me half-eyed,
I might have been his son.

And I remember the musician
Faltering over his fiddle
In Bayswater, London,
He too set me the riddle.

Every old man I see
In October-coloured weather
Seems to say to me:
'I was once your father.'

The Long Garden

It was the garden of the golden apples,
A long garden between a railway and a road,
In the sow's rooting where the hen scratches
We dipped our fingers in the pockets of God.

In the thistly hedge old boots were flying sandals
By which we travelled through the childhood skies,
Old buckets rusty-holed with half-hung handles
Were drums to play when old men married wives.

The pole that lifted the clothes-line in the middle
Was the flag-pole on a prince's palace when
We looked at it through fingers crossed to riddle
In evening sunlight miracles for men.

It was the garden of the golden apples,
And when the Carrick train went by we knew
That we could never die till something happened
Like wishing for a fruit that never grew,

Or wanting to be up on Candle-Fort
Above the village with its shops and mill.
The racing cyclists' gasp-gapped reports
Hinted of pubs where life can drink his fill.

And when the sun went down into Drumcatton
And the New Moon by its little finger swung
From the telegraph wires, we knew how God had happened
And what the blackbird in the whitethorn sang.

It was the garden of the golden apples,
The half-way house where we had stopped a day
Before we took the west road to Drumcatton
Where the sun was always setting on the play.

Art McCooey

I recover now the time I drove
Cart-loads of dung to an outlying farm –
My foreign possessions in Shancoduff –
With the enthusiasm of a man who sees life simply.

The steam rising from the load is still
Warm enough to thaw my frosty fingers.
In Donnybrook in Dublin ten years later
I see that empire now and the empire builder.

Sometimes meeting a neighbour
In country love-enchantment,
The old mare pulls over to the bank and leaves us
To fiddle folly where November dances.

We wove our disappointments and successes
To patterns of a town-bred logic:
'She might have been sick . . . No, never before,
A mystery, Pat, and they all appear so modest.'

We exchanged our fool advices back and forth:
'It easily could be their cow was calving,
And sure the rain was desperate that night . . .'
Somewhere in the mists a light was laughing.

We played with the frilly edges of reality
While we puffed our cigarettes;
And sometimes Owney Martin's splitting yell
Would knife the dreamer that the land begets.

'I'll see you after Second Mass on Sunday.'
'Right-o, right-o.' The mare moves on again.
A wheel rides over a heap of gravel
And the mare goes skew-ways like a blinded hen.

Down the lane-way of the popular banshees
By Paddy Bradley's; mud to the ankles;
A hare is grazing in Mat Rooney's meadow;
Maggie Byrne is prowling for dead branches.

Ten loads before tea-time. Was that the laughter
Of the evening bursting school?
The sun sinks low and large behind the hills of Cavan,
A stormy-looking sunset. 'Brave and cool.'

Wash out the cart with a bucket of water and a wangel
Of wheaten straw. Jupiter looks down.
Unlearnedly and unreasonably poetry is shaped
Awkwardly but alive in the unmeasured womb.

Spraying the Potatoes

The barrels of blue potato-spray
Stood on a headland of July
Beside an orchard wall where roses
Were young girls hanging from the sky.

The flocks of green potato-stalks
Were blossom spread for sudden flight,
The Kerr's Pinks in a frivelled blue,
The Arran Banners wearing white.

And over that potato-field
A hazy veil of woven sun.
Dandelions growing on headlands, showing
Their unloved hearts to everyone.

And I was there with the knapsack sprayer
On the barrel's edge poised. A wasp was floating
Dead on a sunken briar leaf
Over a copper-poisoned ocean.

The axle-roll of a rut-locked cart
Broke the burnt stick of noon in two.
An old man came through a cornfield
Remembering his youth and some Ruth he knew.

He turned my way. 'God further the work.'
He echoed an ancient farming prayer.
I thanked him. He eyed the potato-drills.
He said: 'You are bound to have good ones there.'

We talked and our talk was a theme of kings,
A theme for strings. He hunkered down
In the shade of the orchard wall. O roses
The old man dies in the young girl's frown.

And poet lost to potato-fields,
Remembering the lime and copper smell
Of the spraying barrels he is not lost
Or till blossomed stalks cannot weave a spell.

Memory of Brother Michael

It would never be morning, always evening,
Golden sunset, golden age –
When Shakespeare, Marlowe and Jonson were writing
The future of England page by page
A nettle-wild grave was Ireland's stage.

It would never be spring, always autumn
After a harvest always lost,
When Drake was winning seas for England
We sailed in puddles of the past
Chasing the ghost of Brendan's mast.

The seeds among the dust were less than dust,
Dust we sought, decay,
The young sprout rising smothered in it,
Cursed for being in the way –
And the same is true today.

Culture is always something that was,
Something pedants can measure,
Skull of bard, thigh of chief,
Depth of dried-up river.
Shall we be thus for ever?
Shall we be thus for ever?

Innocence

They laughed at one I loved –
The triangular hill that hung
Under the Big Forth. They said
That I was bounded by the whitethorn hedges
Of the little farm and did not know the world.
But I knew that love's doorway to life
Is the same doorway everywhere.

Ashamed of what I loved
I flung her from me and called her a ditch
Although she was smiling at me with violets.

But now I am back in her briary arms
The dew of an Indian Summer morning lies
On bleached potato-stalks –
What age am I?

I do not know what age I am,
I am no mortal age;
I know nothing of women,

Nothing of cities,
I cannot die
Unless I walk outside these whitethorn hedges.

Prelude

Give us another poem, he said
Or they will think your muse is dead;
Another middle-age departure
Of Apollo from the trade of archer.
Bring out a book as soon as you can
To let them see you're a living man,
Whose comic spirit is untamed
Though sadness for a little claimed
The precedence; and tentative
You pulled your punch and wondered if
Old Cunning Silence might not be
A better bet than poetry.

You have not got the countenance
To hold the angle of pretence,
That angry bitter look for one
Who knows that art's a kind of fun;
That all true poems laugh inwardly
Out of grief-born intensity.
Dullness alone can get you beat
And so can humour's counterfeit.
You have not got a chance with fraud
And might as well be true to God.

Then link your laughter out of doors
In sunlight past the sick-faced whores
Who chant the praise of love that isn't
And bring their bastards to be Christened
At phoney founts by bogus priests
With rites mugged up by journalists
Walk past professors looking serious
Fondling an unpublished thesis –
'A child! my child! my darling son'
Some Poets of Nineteen Hundred and One.

Note well the face profoundly grave,
An empty mind can house a knave.
Be careful to show no defiance,
They've made pretence into a science;
Card-sharpers of the art committee
Working all the provincial cities,
They cry 'Eccentric' if they hear
A voice that seems at all sincere.
Fold up their table and their gear
And with the money disappear.

But satire is unfruitful prayer,
Only wild shoots of pity there,
And you must go inland and be
Lost in compassion's ecstasy,
Where suffering soars in summer air –
The millstone has become a star.

Count then your blessings, hold in mind
All that has loved you or been kind:
Those women on their mercy missions,
Rescue work with kiss or kitchens,
Perceiving through the comic veil
The poet's spirit in travail.
Gather the bits of road that were
Not gravel to the traveller
But eternal lanes of joy
On which no man who walks can die.
Bring in the particular trees
That caught you in their mysteries,
And love again the weeds that grew
Somewhere specially for you.
Collect the river and the stream
That flashed upon a pensive theme,
And a positive world make,
A world man's world cannot shake.
And do not lose love's resolution
Though face to face with destitution.
If Platitude should claim a place
Do not denounce his humble face;
His sentiments are well intentioned
He has a part in the larger legend.

So now my gentle tiger burning
In the forest of no-yearning
Walk on serenely, do not mind
That Promised Land you thought to find,
Where the worldly-wise and rich take over

The mundane problems of the lower,
Ignore Power's schismatic sect,
Lovers alone lovers protect.

Kerr's Ass

We borrowed the loan of Kerr's big ass
To go to Dundalk with butter,
Brought him home the evening before the market
An exile that night in Mucker.

We heeled up the cart before the door,
We took the harness inside –
The straw-stuffed straddle, the broken breeching
With bits of bull-wire tied;

The winkers that had no choke-band,
The collar and the reins . . .
In Ealing Broadway, London Town
I name their several names

Until a world comes to life –
Morning, the silent bog,
And the God of imagination waking
In a Mucker fog.

Epic

I have lived in important places, times
When great events were decided, who owned
That half a rood of rock, a no-man's land
Surrounded by our pitchfork-armed claims.
I heard the Duffys shouting 'Damn your soul'
And old McCabe stripped to the waist, seen
Step the plot defying blue cast-steel –
'Here is the march along these iron stones'.
That was the year of the Munich bother. Which
Was more important? I inclined
To lose my faith in Ballyrush and Gortin
Till Homer's ghost came whispering to my mind.
He said: I made the Iliad from such
A local row. Gods make their own importance.

The Hospital

A year ago I fell in love with the functional ward
Of a chest hospital: square cubicles in a row
Plain concrete, wash basins – an art lover's woe,
Not counting how the fellow in the next bed snored.
But nothing whatever is by love debarred,
The common and banal her heat can know.
The corridor led to a stairway and below
Was the inexhaustible adventure of a gravelled yard.

This is what love does to things: the Rialto Bridge,
The main gate that was bent by a heavy lorry,
The seat at the back of a shed that was a suntrap.
Naming these things is the love-act and its pledge;
For we must record love's mystery without claptrap,
Snatch out of time the passionate transitory.

Come Dance with Kitty Stobling

No, no, no, I know I was not important as I moved
Through the colourful country, I was but a single
Item in the picture, the namer not the beloved.
O tedious man with whom no gods commingle.
Beauty, who has described beauty? Once upon a time
I had a myth that was a lie but it served:
Trees walking across the crests of hills and my rhyme
Cavorting on mile-high stilts and the unnerved
Crowds looking up with terror in their rational faces.
O dance with Kitty Stobling I outrageously
Cried out-of-sense to them, while their timorous paces
Stumbled behind Jove's page boy paging me.
I had a very pleasant journey, thank you sincerely
For giving me my madness back, or nearly.

In Memory of my Mother

I do not think of you lying in the wet clay
Of a Monaghan graveyard; I see
You walking down a lane among the poplars
On your way to the station, or happily

Going to second Mass on a summer Sunday –
You meet me and you say:
'Don't forget to see about the cattle –'
Among your earthiest words the angels stray.

And I think of you walking along a headland
Of green oats in June,
So full of repose, so rich with life –
And I see us meeting at the end of a town

On a fair day by accident, after
The bargains are all made and we can walk
Together through the shops and stalls and markets
Free in the oriental streets of thought.

O you are not lying in the wet clay,
For it is a harvest evening now and we
Are piling up the ricks against the moonlight
And you smile up at us – eternally.

LOUIS MACNEICE   1907–1963

River in Spate

The river falls and over the walls the coffins of cold funerals
Slide deep and sleep there in the close tomb of the pool,
And yellow waters lave the grave and pebbles pave
                                        its mortuary
And the river horses vault and plunge with their assault
                                        and battery,
And helter-skelter the coffins come and the drums beat and
                                        the waters flow,
And the panther horses lift their hooves and paw and shift
                                        and draw the bier,
The corpses blink in the rush of the river, and out of the
                                        water their chins they tip
And quaff the gush and lip the draught and crook their
                                        heads and crow,
Drowned and drunk with the cataract that carries them
                                        and buries them
And silts them over and covers them and lilts and chuckles
                                        over their bones;
The organ-tones that the winds raise will never pierce
                                        the water ways,
So all they will hear is the fall of hooves and the distant
                                        shake of harness,
And the beat of the bells on the horses' heads and the
                                        undertaker's laughter,
And the murmur that will lose its strength and blur at
                                        length to quietness,
And afterwards the minute heard descending,
                                        never ending heard,
And then the minute after and the minute after the minute
                                        after.

Sunday Morning

Down the road someone is practising scales,
The notes like little fishes vanish with a wink of tails,
Man's heart expands to tinker with his car
For this is Sunday morning, Fate's great bazaar;
Regard these means as ends, concentrate on this Now,
And you may grow to music or drive beyond Hindhead
                                     anyhow,
Take corners on two wheels until you go so fast
That you can clutch a fringe or two of the windy past,
That you can abstract this day and make it to the week of
                                     time
A small eternity, a sonnet self-contained in rhyme.

But listen, up the road, something gulps, the church spire
Opens its eight bells out, skulls' mouths which will not tire
To tell how there is no music or movement which secures
Escape from the weekday time. Which deadens and
                                     endures.

Train to Dublin

Our half-thought thoughts divide in sifted wisps
Against the basic facts repatterned without pause,
I can no more gather my mind up in my fist
Than the shadow of the smoke of this train upon the grass –
This is the way that animals' lives pass.

The train's rhythm never relents, the telephone posts
Go striding backwards like the legs of time to where
In a Georgian house you turn at the carpet's edge
Turning a sentence while, outside my window here,
The smoke makes broken queries in the air.

The train keeps moving and the rain holds off,
I count the buttons on the seat, I hear a shell
Held hollow to the ear, the mere
Reiteration of integers, the bell
That tolls and tolls, the monotony of fear.

At times we are doctrinaire, at times we are frivolous,
Plastering over the cracks, a gesture making good,
But the strength of us does not come out of us.
It is we, I think, are the idols and it is God
Has set us up as men who are painted wood,

And the trains carry us about. But not consistently so,
For during a tiny portion of our lives we are not in trains,
The idol living for a moment, not muscle-bound
But walking freely through the slanting rain,
Its ankles wet, its grimace relaxed again.

[83]

All over the world people are toasting the King,
Red lozenges of light as each one lifts his glass,
But I will not give you any idol or idea, creed or king,
I give you the incidental things which pass
Outward through space exactly as each was.

I give you the disproportion between labour spent
And joy at random; the laughter of the Galway sea
Juggling with spars and bones irresponsibly,
I give you the toy Liffey and the vast gulls,
I give you fuchsia hedges and whitewashed walls.

I give you the smell of Norman stone, the squelch
Of bog beneath your boots, the red bog-grass,
The vivid chequer of the Antrim hills, the trough of dark
Golden water for the cart-horses, the brass
Belt of serene sun upon the lough.

And I give you the faces, not the permanent masks,
But the faces balanced in the toppling wave –
His glint of joy in cunning as the farmer asks
Twenty per cent too much, or a girl's, forgetting to be
                                                                    suave,
A tiro choosing stuffs, preferring mauve.

And I give you the sea and yet again the sea's
Tumultuous marble,
With Thor's thunder or taking his ease akimbo,
Lumbering torso, but finger-tips a marvel
Of surgeon's accuracy.

I would like to give you more but I cannot hold
This stuff within my hands and the train goes on;
I know that there are further syntheses to which,
As you have perhaps, people at last attain
And find that they are rich and breathing gold.

Snow

The room was suddenly rich and the great bay-window was
Spawning snow and pink roses against it
Soundlessly collateral and incompatible:
World is suddener than we fancy it.

World is crazier and more of it than we think,
Incorrigibly plural. I peel and portion
A tangerine and spit the pips and feel
The drunkenness of things being various.

And the fire flames with a bubbling sound for world
Is more spiteful and gay than one supposes –
On the tongue on the eyes on the ears in the palms of one's
                                                    hands –
There is more than glass between the snow and the huge
                                                    roses.

Eclogue between the Motherless

A: What did you do for the holiday?
B: I went home.
    What did you do?
A: O, I went home for the holiday.
    Had a good time?
B: Not bad as far as it went.
    What about you?
A: O quite a good time on the whole –
BOTH: Quite a good time on the whole at home for the
                                                    holiday

A: As far as it went – In a way it went too far,
    Back to childhood, back to the backwoods mind;
    I could not stand a great deal of it, bars on the brain
    And the blinds drawn in the drawing-room not to
                                        fade the chair covers
B: There were no blinds drawn in ours; my father has
                                            married again –
    A girl of thirty who had never had any lovers
    And wants to have everything bright
A: That sounds worse than us.
    Our old house is just a grass-grown tumulus
    My father sits by himself with the bossed decanter,
    The garden is going to rack, the gardener
    Only comes three days, most of our money was in
                                                    linen
B: My new stepmother is wealthy, you should see her
                                            in jodhpurs
    Brisking in to breakfast from a morning canter.

I don't think he can be happy

A: How can you tell?
That generation is so different

B: I suppose your sister
Still keeps house for yours?

A: Yes and she finds it hell.
Nothing to do in the evenings.

B: Talking of the evenings
I can drop the ash on the carpet since my divorce.
Never you marry, my boy. One marries only
Because one thinks one is lonely – and so one was
But wait till the lonely are two and no better

A: As a matter
Of fact I've got to tell you

B: The first half year
Is heaven come back from the nursery – swansdown
             kisses –
But after that one misses something

A: My dear,
Don't depress me in advance; I've got to tell you –

B: My wife was warmth, a picture and a dance,
Her body electric – silk used to crackle and her gloves
Move where she left them. How one loves the surface
But how one lacks the core – Children of course
Might make a difference

A: Personally I find
I cannot go on any more like I was. Which is why
I took this step in the dark

B: What step?

A: I thought
   I too might try what you
B: Don't say that you
   And after all this time
A: Let's start from the start.
   When I went home this time there was nothing to do
   And so I got haunted. Like a ball of wool
   That kittens have got at, all my growing up
   All the disposed-of process of my past
   Unravelled on the floor – One can't proceed any more
   Except on a static past; when the ice-floe breaks
   What's the good of walking? Talking of ice
   I remembered my mother standing against the sky
   And saying 'Go back in the house and change your
                                                    shoes'
   And I kept having dreams and kept going back in the
                                                    house.
   A sense of guilt like a scent – The day I was born
   I suppose that that same hour was full of her screams
B: You're run down
A: Wait till you hear what I've done.
   It was not only dreams; even the crockery (odd
   It's not all broken by now) and the rustic seat in the
                                                    rockery
   With the bark flaked off, all kept reminding me,
                                                    binding
   My feet to the floating past. In the night at the lodge
   A dog was barking as when I was little in the night

And I could not budge in the bed clothes. Lying alone
I felt my legs were paralysed into roots
And the same cracks in what used to be the nursery
ceiling
Gave me again the feeling I was young among ikons,
Helpless at the feet of faceless family idols,
Walking the tightrope over the tiger-pit,
Running the gauntlet of inherited fears;
So after all these years I turned in the bed
And grasped the want of a wife and heard in the rain
On the gravel path the steps of all my mistresses
And wondered which was coming or was she dead
And her shoes given to the char which tapped through
London –
The black streets mirrored with rain and stained with
lights.
I dreamed she came while a train
Was running behind the trees (with power progressing),
Undressing deftly she slipped cool knees beside me,
The clipped hair on her neck prickled my tongue
And the whole room swung like a ship till I woke
with the window
Jittering in its frame from the train passing the garden
Carrying its load of souls to a different distance.
And of others, isolated by associations,
I thought – the scent of syringa or always wearing
A hat of fine white straw and never known in winter –
Splinters of memory. When I was little I sorted

Bits of lustre and glass from the heap behind the hen-
house;
They are all distorted now the beautiful sirens
Mutilated and mute in dream's dissection,
Hanged from pegs in the Bluebeard's closet of the
brain,
Never again nonchalantly to open
The doors of disillusion. Whom recording
The night marked time, the dog at the lodge kept
barking
And as he barked the big cave opened of hell
Where all their voices were one and stuck at a point
Like a gramophone needle stuck on a notched record.
I thought 'Can I find a love beyond the family
And feed her to the bed my mother died in
Between the tallboys and the vase of honesty
On which I was born and groped my way from the cave
With a half-eaten fruit in my hand, a passport meaning
Enforced return for periods to that country?
Or will one's wife also belong to that country
And can one never find the perfect stranger?'
B: My complaint was that she stayed a stranger.
I remember her mostly in the car, stopping by the
white
Moons of the petrol pumps, in a camelhair rug
Comfortable, scented and alien.
A: That's what I want,
Someone immutably alien –
Send me a woman with haunches out of the jungle

[90]

And frost patterns for fancies,
The hard light of sun upon water in diamonds
                                        dancing
And the brute swagger of the sea; let her love be the
                                        drop
From the cliff of my dream, be the axe on the block
Be finesse of the ice on the panes of the heart
Be careless, be callous, be glass frolic of prisms,
Be eyes of guns through lashes of barbed wire,
Be the gaoler's smile and all that breaks the past.
B: Odd ideals you have; all I wanted
Was to get really close but closeness was
Only a glove on the hand, alien and veinless,
And yet her empty gloves could move
A: My next move
Is what I've got to tell you, I picked on the only
One who would suit and wrote proposing marriage
B: Who is she?
A: But she can't have yet received it;
She is in India.
B: India be damned.
What is her name?
A: I said I cannot offer
Anything you will want
B: Why?
A: and I said
I know in two years' time it will make no difference.
I was hardly able to write it at the claw-foot table
Where my mother kept her diary. There I sat

Concocting a gambler's medicine; the afternoon was
                                                    cool,
The ducks drew lines of white on the dull slate of the
                                                    pool
And I sat writing to someone I hardly knew
And someone I shall never know well. Relying on
                                                    that
I stuck up the envelope, walked down the winding
                                                    drive,
All that was wanted a figurehead, passed by the
                                                    lodge
Where the dog is chained and the gates, relying on
                                                    my mood
To get it posted
B: Who is the woman?
A: relying
B: Who is the woman?
A: She is dying
B: Dying of what?
A: Only a year to live
B: Forgive me asking
But
A: Only a year and ten yards down the road
I made my goal where it has always stood
Waiting for the last
B: You must be out of your mind;
If it were anyone else I should not mind
A: Waiting for the last collection before dark
The pillarbox like an exclamation mark.

Valediction

Their verdure dare not show . . . their verdure dare not
show . . .
Cant and randy – the seals' heads bobbing in the tide-flow
Between the islands, sleek and black and irrelevant
They cannot depose logically what they want:
Died by gunshot under borrowed pennons,
Sniped from the wet gorse and taken by the limp fins
And slung like a dead seal in a boghole, beaten up
By peasants with long lips and the whisky-drinker's cough.
Park your car in the city of Dublin, see Sackville Street
Without the sandbags in the old photos, meet
The statues of the patriots, history never dies,
At any rate in Ireland, arson and murder are legacies
Like old rings hollow-eyed without their stones
Dumb talismans.
See Belfast, devout and profane and hard,
Built on reclaimed mud, hammers playing in the shipyard,
Time punched with holes like a steel sheet, time
Hardening the faces, veneering with a grey and speckled
rime
The faces under the shawls and caps:
This was my mother-city, these my paps.
Country of callous lava cooled to stone,
Of minute sodden haycocks, of ship-sirens' moan,
Of falling intonations – I would call you to book
I would say to you, Look;
I would say, This is what you have given me
Indifference and sentimentality
A metallic giggle, a fumbling hand,

A heart that leaps to a fife band:
Set these against your water-shafted air
Of amethyst and moonstone, the horses' feet like bells of
                                           hair
Shambling beneath the orange cart, the beer-brown spring
Guzzling between the heather, the green gush of Irish
                                           spring.
Cursèd be he that curses his mother. I cannot be
Anyone else than what this land engendered me:
In the back of my mind are snips of white, the sails
Of the Lough's fishing-boats, the bellropes lash their tails
When I would peal my thoughts, the bells pull free –
Memory in apostasy.
I would tot up my factors
But who can stand in the way of his soul's steam-tractors?
I can say Ireland is hooey, Ireland is
A gallery of fake tapestries,
But I cannot deny my past to which my self is wed,
The woven figure cannot undo its thread.
On a cardboard lid I saw when I was four
Was the trade-mark of a hound and a round tower,
And that was Irish glamour, and in the cemetery
Sham Celtic crosses claimed our individuality,
And my father talked about the West where years back
He played hurley on the sands with a stick of wrack.
Park your car in Killarney, buy a souvenir
Of green marble or black bog-oak, run up to Clare,
Climb the cliff in the postcard, visit Galway city,
Romanticize on our Spanish blood, leave ten per cent of
                                           pity
Under your plate for the emigrant,

Take credit for our sanctity, our heroism and our sterile
                                                        want
Columba Kevin and briny Brandan the accepted names,
Wolfe Tone and Grattan and Michael Collins the accepted
                                                        names,
Admire the suavity with which the architect
Is rebuilding the burnt mansion, recollect
The palmy days of the Horse Show, swank your fill,
But take the Holyhead boat before you pay the bill;
Before you face the consequence
Of inbred soul and climatic maleficence
And pay for the trick beauty of a prism
In drug-dull fatalism.
I will exorcise my blood
And not to have my baby-clothes my shroud
I will acquire an attitude not yours
And become as one of your holiday visitors,
And however often I may come
Farewell, my country, and in perpetuum;
Whatever desire I catch when your wind scours my face
I will take home and put in a glass case
And merely look on
At each new fantasy of badge and gun.
Frost will not touch the hedge of fuchsias,
The land will remain as it was,
But no abiding content can grow out of these minds
Fuddled with blood, always caught by blinds;
The eels go up the Shannon over the great dam;
You cannot change a response by giving it a new name.
Fountain of green and blue curling in the wind
I must go east and stay, not looking behind,
Not knowing on which day the mist is blanket-thick

Nor when sun quilts the valley and quick
Winging shadows of white clouds pass
Over the long hills like a fiddle's phrase.
If I were a dog of sunlight I would bound
From Phoenix Park to Achill Sound,
Picking up the scent of a hundred fugitives
That have broken the mesh of ordinary lives,
But being ordinary too I must in course discuss
What we mean to Ireland or Ireland to us;
I have to observe milestone and curio
The beaten buried gold of an old king's bravado,
Falsetto antiquities, I have to gesture,
Take part in, or renounce, each imposture;
Therefore I resign, good-bye the chequered and the quiet
                                          hills

The gaudily-striped Atlantic, the linen-mills
That swallow the shawled file, the black moor where half
A turf-stack stands like a ruined cenotaph;
Good-bye your hens running in and out of the white house
Your absent-minded goats along the road, your black cows
Your greyhounds and your hunters beautifully bred
Your drums and your dolled-up Virgins and your ignorant
                                          dead.

Carrickfergus

I was born in Belfast between the mountain and the
                                                    gantries
    To the hooting of lost sirens and the clang of trams:
Thence to Smoky Carrick in County Antrim
    Where the bottle-neck harbour collects the mud which
                                                    jams

The little boats beneath the Norman castle,
    The pier shining with lumps of crystal salt;
The Scotch Quarter was a line of residential houses
    But the Irish Quarter was a slum for the blind and halt.

The brook ran yellow from the factory stinking of chlorine,
    The yarn-mill called its funeral cry at noon;
Our lights looked over the lough to the lights of Bangor
    Under the peacock aura of a drowning moon.

The Norman walled this town against the country
    To stop his ears to the yelping of his slave
And built a church in the form of a cross but denoting
    The list of Christ on the cross in the angle of the nave.

I was the rector's son, born to the anglican order,
    Banned for ever from the candles of the Irish poor;
The Chichesters knelt in marble at the end of a transept
    With ruffs about their necks, their portion sure.

The war came and a huge camp of soldiers
  Grew from the ground in sight of our house with long
Dummies hanging from gibbets for bayonet practice
  And the sentry's challenge echoing all day long;

A Yorkshire terrier ran in and out by the gate-lodge
  Barred to civilians, yapping as if taking affront:
Marching at ease and singing 'Who Killed Cock Robin?'
  The troops went out by the lodge and off to the Front.

The steamer was camouflaged that took me to England –
  Sweat and khaki in the Carlisle train;
I thought that the war would last for ever and sugar
  Be always rationed and that never again

Would the weekly papers not have photos of sandbags
  And my governess not make bandages from moss
And people not have maps above the fireplace
  With flags on pins moving across and across –

Across the hawthorn hedge the noise of bugles,
  Flares across the night,
Somewhere on the lough was a prison ship for Germans,
  A cage across their sight.

I went to school in Dorset, the world of parents
  Contracted into a puppet world of sons
Far from the mill girls, the smell of porter, the salt-mines
  And the soldiers with their guns.

The Brandy Glass

Only let it form within his hands once more –
The moment cradled like a brandy glass.
Sitting alone in the empty dining hall . . .
From the chandeliers the snow begins to fall
Piling around carafes and table legs
And chokes the passage of the revolving door.
The last diner, like a ventriloquist's doll
Left by his master, gazes before him, begs:
'Only let it form within my hands once more.'

from Autumn Journal

XVI

Nightmare leaves fatigue:
    We envy men of action
Who sleep and wake, murder and intrigue
    Without being doubtful, without being haunted.
And I envy the intransigence of my own
    Countrymen who shoot to kill and never
See the victim's face become their own
    Or find his motive sabotage their motives.
So reading the memoirs of Maud Gonne,
    Daughter of an English mother and a soldier father,
I note how a single purpose can be founded on
    A jumble of opposites:

[99]

Dublin Castle, the vice-regal ball,
  The embassies of Europe,
Hatred scribbled on a wall,
  Gaols and revolvers.
And I remember, when I was little, the fear
  Bandied among the servants
That Casement would land at the pier
  With a sword and a horde of rebels;
And how we used to expect, at a later date,
  When the wind blew from the west, the noise of shooting
Starting in the evening at eight
  In Belfast in the York Street district;
And the voodoo of the Orange bands
  Drawing an iron net through darkest Ulster,
Flailing the limbo lands –
  The linen mills, the long wet grass, the ragged hawthorn.
And one read black where the other read white, his hope
  The other man's damnation:
Up the Rebels, To Hell with the Pope,
  And God Save – as you prefer – the King or Ireland.
The land of scholars and saints:
  Scholars and saints my eye, the land of ambush,
Purblind manifestoes, never-ending complaints,
  The born martyr and the gallant ninny;
The grocer drunk with the drum,
  The land-owner shot in his bed, the angry voices
Piercing the broken fanlight in the slum,
  The shawled woman weeping at the garish altar.
Kathaleen ni Houlihan! Why
  Must a country, like a ship or a car, be always female,
Mother or sweetheart? A woman passing by,
  We did but see her passing.

Passing like a patch of sun on the rainy hill
 And yet we love her for ever and hate our neighbour
And each one in his will
 Binds his heirs to continuance of hatred.
Drums on the haycock, drums on the harvest, black
 Drums in the night shaking the windows:
King William is riding his white horse back
 To the Boyne on a banner.
Thousands of banners, thousands of white
 Horses, thousands of Williams
Waving thousands of swords and ready to fight
 Till the blue sea turns to orange.
Such was my country and I thought I was well
 Out of it, educated and domiciled in England,
Though yet her name keeps ringing like a bell
 In an under-water belfry.
Why do we like being Irish? Partly because
 It gives us a hold on the sentimental English
As members of a world that never was,
 Baptized with fairy water;
And partly because Ireland is small enough
 To be still thought of with a family feeling,
And because the waves are rough
 That split her from a more commercial culture;
And because one feels that here at least one can
 Do local work which is not at the world's mercy
And that on this tiny stage with luck a man
 Might see the end of one particular action.
It is self-deception of course;
 There is no immunity in this island either;
A cart that is drawn by somebody else's horse
 And carrying goods to somebody else's market.

[101]

The bombs in the turnip sack, the sniper from the roof,
   Griffith, Connolly, Collins, where have they brought us?
Ourselves alone! Let the round tower stand aloof
   In a world of bursting mortar!
Let the school-children fumble their sums
   In a half-dead language;
Let the censor be busy on the books; pull down the
                              Georgian slums;
   Let the games be played in Gaelic.
Let them grow beet-sugar; let them build
   A factory in every hamlet;
Let them pigeon-hole the souls of the killed
   Into sheep and goats, patriots and traitors.
And the North, where I was a boy,
   Is still the North, veneered with the grime of Glasgow,
Thousands of men whom nobody will employ
   Standing at the corners, coughing.
And the street-children play on the wet
   Pavement – hopscotch or marbles;
And each rich family boasts a sagging tennis-net
   On a spongy lawn beside a dripping shrubbery.
The smoking chimneys hint
   At prosperity round the corner
But they make their Ulster linen from foreign lint
   And the money that comes in goes out to make more
                                  money.

A city built upon mud;
   A culture built upon profit;
Free speech nipped in the bud,
   The minority always guilty.
Why should I want to go back
   To you, Ireland, my Ireland?

The blots on the page are so black
    That they cannot be covered with shamrock.
I hate your grandiose airs,
    Your sob-stuff, your laugh and your swagger,
Your assumption that everyone cares
    Who is the king of your castle.
Castles are out of date,
    The tide flows round the children's sandy fancy;
Put up what flag you like, it is too late
    To save your soul with bunting.
Odi atque amo:
    Shall we cut this name on trees with a rusty dagger?
Her moutains are still blue, her rivers flow
    Bubbling over the boulders.
She is both a bore and a bitch;
    Better close the horizon,
Send her no more fantasy, no more longings which
    Are under a fatal tariff.
For common sense is the vogue
    And she gives her children neither sense nor money
Who slouch around the world with a gesture and a brogue
    And a faggot of useless memories.

from The Closing Album

II

Cushendun

Fuchsia and ragweed and the distant hills
Made as it were out of clouds and sea:
All night the bay is plashing and the moon
  Marks the break of the waves.

Limestone and basalt and a whitewashed house
With passages of great stone flags
And a walled garden with plums on the wall
  And a bird piping in the night.

Forgetfulness: brass lamps and copper jugs
And home-made bread and the smell of turf or flax
And the air a glove and the water lathering easy
  And convolvulus in the hedge.

Only in the dark green room beside the fire
With the curtains drawn against the winds and waves
There is a little box with a well-bred voice:
  What a place to talk of War.

Meeting Point

Time was away and somewhere else,
There were two glasses and two chairs
And two people with the one pulse
(Somebody stopped the moving stairs):
Time was away and somewhere else.

And they were neither up nor down;
The stream's music did not stop
Flowing through heather, limpid brown,
Although they sat in a coffee shop
And they were neither up nor down.

The bell was silent in the air
Holding its inverted poise –
Between the clang and clang a flower,
A brazen calyx of no noise:
The bell was silent in the air.

The camels crossed the miles of sand
That stretched around the cups and plates;
The desert was their own, they planned
To portion out the stars and dates:
The camels crossed the miles of sand.

Time was away and somewhere else.
The waiter did not come, the clock
Forgot them and the radio waltz
Came out like water from a rock:
Time was away and somewhere else.

Her fingers flicked away the ash
That bloomed again in tropic trees:
Not caring if the markets crash
When they had forests such as these,
Her fingers flicked away the ash.

God or whatever means the Good
Be praised that time can stop like this,
That what the heart has understood
Can verify in the body's peace
God or whatever means the Good.

Time was away and she was here
And life no longer what it was,
The bell was silent in the air
And all the room one glow because
Time was away and she was here.

Novelettes III

The Gardener

He was not able to read or write,
He did odd jobs on gentlemen's places
Cutting the hedge or hoeing the drive
With the smile of a saint,
With the pride of a feudal chief,
For he was not quite all there.

Crippled by rheumatism
By the time his hair was white,
He would reach the garden by twelve
His legs in soiled puttees,
A clay pipe in his teeth,
A tiny flag in his cap,
A white cat behind him,
And his eyes a cornflower blue.

And between the clack of the shears
Or the honing of the scythe
Or the rattle of the rake on the gravel
He would talk to amuse the children,
He would talk to himself or the cat
Or the robin waiting for worms
Perched on the handle of the spade;
Would remember snatches of verse
From the elementary school
About a bee and a wasp
Or the cat by the barndoor spinning;
And would talk about himself for ever –
You would never find his like –
Always in the third person;
And would level his stick like a gun
(With a glint in his eye)
Saying 'Now I'm a Frenchman' –
He was not quite right in the head.

He believed in God –
The Good Fellow Up There –
And he used a simile of Homer
Watching the falling leaves,
And every year he waited for the Twelfth of July,
Cherishing his sash and his fife
For the carnival of banners and drums.
He was always claiming but never
Obtaining his old age pension,
For he did not know his age.

And his rheumatism at last
Kept him out of the processions.
And he came to work in the garden
Later and later in the day,
Leaving later at night;
In the damp dark of the night
At ten o'clock or later
You could hear him mowing the lawn,
The mower moving forward,
And backward, forward and backward
For he mowed while standing still;
He was not quite up to the job.

But he took a pride in the job,
He kept a bowl of cold
Tea in the crotch of a tree,
Always enjoyed his food
And enjoyed honing the scythe
And making the potato drills
And putting the peasticks in;
And enjoyed the noise of the corncrake,
And the early hawthorn hedge
Peppered black and green,
And the cut grass dancing in the air –
Happy as the day was long.

Till his last sickness took him
And he could not leave his house
And his eyes lost their colour
And he sat by the little range
With a finch in a cage and a framed
Certificate of admission
Into the Orange Order,
And his speech began to wander
And memory ebbed
Leaving upon the shore
Odd shells and heads of wrack
And his soul went out on the ebbing
Tide in a trim boat
To find the Walls of Derry
Or the land of the Ever Young.

Flight of the Heart

Heart, my heart, what will you do?
There are five lame dogs and one deaf-mute
All of them with demands on you.

I will build myself a copper tower
With four ways out and no way in
But mine the glory, mine the power.

And what if the tower should shake and fall
With three sharp taps and one big bang?
What would you do with yourself at all?

I would go in the cellar and drink the dark
With two quick sips and one long pull,
Drunk as a lord and gay as a lark.

But what when the cellar roof caves in
With one blue flash and nine old bones?
How, my heart, will you save your skin?

I will go back where I belong
With one foot first and both eyes blind
I will go back where I belong
In the fore-being of mankind.

Autobiography

In my childhood trees were green
And there was plenty to be seen.

Come back early or never come.

My father made the walls resound,
He wore his collar the wrong way round.

Come back early or never come.

My mother wore a yellow dress;
Gently, gently, gentleness.

Come back early or never come.

When I was five the black dreams came;
Nothing after was quite the same.

Come back early or never come.

The dark was talking to the dead;
The lamp was dark beside my bed.

Come back early or never come.

When I woke they did not care;
Nobody, nobody was there.

Come back early or never come.

When my silent terror cried,
Nobody, nobody replied.

Come back early or never come.

I got up; the chilly sun
Saw me walk away alone.

Come back early or never come.

Prayer before Birth

I am not yet born; O hear me.
Let not the bloodsucking bat or the rat or the stoat or the
    club-footed ghoul come near me.

I am not yet born, console me.
I fear that the human race may with tall walls wall me,
    with strong drugs dope me, with wise lies lure me,
        on black racks rack me, in blood-baths roll me.

I am not yet born; provide me
With water to dandle me, grass to grow for me, trees to talk
    to me, sky to sing to me, birds and a white light
        in the back of my mind to guide me.

I am not yet born; forgive me
For the sins that in me the world shall commit, my words
    when they speak me, my thoughts when they think me,
        my treason engendered by traitors beyond me,
           my life when they murder by means of my
              hands, my death when they live me.

I am not yet born; rehearse me
In the parts I must play and the cues I must take when
    old men lecture me, bureaucrats hector me, mountains
        frown at me, lovers laugh at me, the white
           waves call me to folly and the desert calls
              me to doom and the beggar refuses
                  my gift and my children curse me.

I am not yet born; O hear me,
Let not the man who is beast or who thinks he is God
    come near me.

I am not yet born; O fill me
With strength against those who would freeze my
    humanity, would dragoon me into a lethal automaton,
        would make me a cog in a machine, a thing with
           one face, a thing, and against all those
              who would dissipate my entirety, would
                blow me like thistledown hither and
                  thither or hither and thither
                    like water held in the
                      hands would spill me.

Let them not make me a stone and let them not spill me.
Otherwise kill me.

Epitaph for Liberal Poets

If in the latter
End – which is fairly soon – our way of life goes west
And some shall say *So What* and some *What Matter*,
Ready under new names to exploit or be exploited,
What, though better unsaid, would we have history say
Of us who walked in our sleep and died on our Quest?

We who always had, but never admitted, a master,
Who were expected – and paid – to be ourselves,
Conditioned to think freely, how can we
Patch up our broken hearts and modes of thought in

plaster

And glorify in chromium-plated stories
Those who shall supersede us and cannot need us –
The tight-lipped technocratic Conquistadores?

The Individual has died before; Catullus
Went down young, gave place to those who were born old
And more adaptable and were not even jealous
Of his wild life and lyrics. Though our songs
Were not so warm as his, our fate is no less cold.

Such silence then before us, pinned against the wall,
Why need we whine? There is no way out, the birds
Will tell us nothing more; we shall vanish first,
Yet leave behind us certain frozen words
Which some day, though not certainly, may melt
And, for a moment or two, accentuate a thirst.

Under the Mountain

Seen from above
The foam in the curving bay is a goose-quill
That feathers . . . unfeathers . . . itself.

Seen from above
The field is a flap and the haycocks buttons
To keep it flush with the earth.

Seen from above
The house is a silent gadget whose purpose
Was long since obsolete.

But when you get down
The breakers are cold scum and the wrack
Sizzles with stinking life.

When you get down
The field is a failed or a worth-while crop, the source
Of back-ache if not heartache.

And when you get down
The house is a maelstrom of loves and hates where you –
Having got down – belong.

Woods

My father who found the English landscape tame
Had hardly in his life walked in a wood,
Too old when first he met one; Malory's knights,
Keats's nymphs or the Midsummer Night's Dream
Could never arras the room, where he spelled out True
                                                and Good
With their interleaving of half-truths and not-quites.

While for me from the age of ten the socketed wooden gate
Into a Dorset planting, into a dark
But gentle ambush, was an alluring eye;
Within was a kingdom free from time and sky,
Caterpillar webs on the forehead, danger under the feet,
And the mind adrift in a floating and rustling ark

Packed with birds and ghosts, two of every race,
Trills of love from the picture-book – Oh might I never
                                                land
But here, grown six foot tall, find me also a love
Also out of the picture-book; whose hand
Would be soft as the webs of the wood and on her face
The wood-pigeon's voice would shaft a chrism from
                                                above.

So in a grassy ride a rain-filled hoof-mark coined
By a finger of sun from the mint of Long Ago
Was the last of Lancelot's glitter. Make-believe dies hard;
That the rider passed here lately and is a man we know
Is still untrue, the gate to Legend remains unbarred,
The grown-up hates to divorce what the child joined.

Thus from a city when my father would frame
Escape, he thought, as I do, of bog or rock
But I have also this other, this English, choice
Into what yet is foreign; whatever its name
Each wood is the mystery and the recurring shock
Of its dark coolness is a foreign voice.

Yet in using the word tame my father was maybe right,
These woods are not the Forest; each is moored
To a village somewhere near. If not of today
They are not like the wilds of Mayo, they are assured
Of their place by men; reprieved from the neolithic night
By gamekeepers or by Herrick's girls at play.

And always we walk out again. The patch
Of sky at the end of the path grows and discloses
An ordered open air long ruled by dyke and fence,
With geese whose form and gait proclaim their
                                                consequence,
Pargetted outposts, windows browed with thatch,
And cow pats – and inconsequent wild roses.

Elegy for Minor Poets

Who often found their way to pleasant meadows
Or maybe once to a peak, who saw the Promised Land,
Who took the correct three strides but tripped their
                                                    hurdles,
Who had some prompter they barely could understand,
Who were too happy or sad, too soon or late,
I would praise these in company with the Great;

For if not in the same way, they fingered the same
                                                    language
According to their lights. For them as for us
Chance was a coryphaeus who could be either
An angel or an *ignus fatuus*.
Let us keep our mind open, our fingers crossed;
Some who go dancing through dark bogs are lost.

Who were lost in many ways, through comfort, lack of
                                                    knowledge,
Or between women's breasts, who thought too little, too
                                                    much,
Who were the world's best talkers, in tone and rhythm
Superb, yet as writers lacked a sense of touch,
So either gave up or just went on and on –
Let us salute them now their chance is gone;

And give the benefit of the doubtful summer
To those who worshipped the sky but stayed indoors
Bound to a desk by conscience or by the spirit's
Hayfever. From those office and study floors
Let the sun clamber on to the notebook, shine,
And fill in what they groped for between each line.

Who were too carefree or careful, who were too many
Though always few and alone, who went the pace
But ran in circles, who were lamed by fashion,
Who lived in the wrong time or the wrong place,
Who might have caught fire had only a spark occurred,
Who knew all the words but failed to achieve the Word –

Their ghosts are gagged, their books are library flotsam,
Some of their names – not all – we learnt in school
But, life being short, we rarely read their poems,
Mere source-books now to point or except a rule,
While those opinions which rank them high are based
On a wish to be different or on lack of taste.

In spite of and because of which, we later
Suitors to their mistress (who, unlike them, stays young)
Do right to hang on the grave of each a trophy
Such as, if solvent, he would himself have hung
Above himself; these debtors preclude our scorn –
Did we not underwrite them when we were born?

Slow Movement

Waking, he found himself in a train, andante,
With wafers of early sunlight blessing the unknown fields
And yesterday cancelled out, except for yesterday's papers
    Huddling under the seat.

It is still very early, this is a slow movement;
The viola-player's hand like a fish in a glass tank
Rises, remains quivering, darts away
    To nibble invisible weeds.

Great white nebulae lurch against the window
To deploy across the valley, the children are not yet up
To wave us on – we pass without spectators,
    Braiding a voiceless creed.

And the girl opposite, name unknown, is still
Asleep and the colour of her eyes unknown
Which might be wells of sun or moons of wish
    But it is still very early.

The movement ends, the train has come to a stop
In buttercup fields, the fiddles are silent, the whole
Shoal of silver tessellates the aquarium
    Floor, not a bubble rises . . .

And what happens next on the programme we do not know,
If, the red line topped on the gauge, the fish will go mad in
    the tank
Accelerando con forza, the sleeper open her eyes
    And, so doing, open ours.

from Autumn Sequel

Canto IV

To work. To my own office, my own job,
Not matching pictures but inventing sound,
Precalculating microphone and knob

In homage to the human voice. To found
A castle on the air requires a mint
Of golden intonations and a mound

Of typescript in the trays. What was in print
Must take on breath and what was thought be said.
In the end there was the Word, at first a glint,

Then an illumination overhead
Where the high towers are lit. Such was our aim
But aims too often languish and instead

We hack and hack. What ought to soar and flame
Shies at its take-off, all our kites collapse,
Our spirit leaks away, our notes are tame,

The castle is on the carpet, aisle and apse
Are shrunk to this small office where large files
Reproach me and a typewriter taps and taps.

Shorthand and a new ribbon; miles on miles
Of carbon copies rippling through the waste
Of office hours that no red light beguiles;

The Word takes shape elsewhere and carapaced
Administrators crouch on constant guard
To save it for good business and good taste.

A seven-figure audience makes things hard
Because they want things easy; as Harrap said
Suggesting I might make an air-borne bard

(Who spoke in parentheses and now is dead),
'On the one hand – as a matter of fact I should
Say on the first hand – there is daily bread,

At least I assume there is, to be made good
If good is the right expression; on the other
Or one of the other hands there is much dead wood

On the air in a manner of speaking which tends to smother
What spark you start with; nevertheless although
Frustration is endemic (take my brother,

He simply thinks me mad to bother so
With people by the million) nevertheless
Our work is aimed at one at a time, you know,

And by and large and at an approximate guess
If poets must live (perhaps I am wrong to think
They must but if they must) they might find this mess

No more a mess than wasting wits and ink
On scratching each other's backs or possibly eyes
Out or half out (no wonder they take to drink;

We might have one by the way) but it could arise
They found it in fact less messy; after all
Homer liked words aloud.' Harrap's blue eyes

Twinkled between the brackets, a silver ball
Darted about the pin-table as he leant
Over the bar. Remembering that Saul

Was also among the prophets and that the rent
Had to be paid and that what Harrap half
Or three and a half times said, he singly meant,

And that some grain is better than no chaff
And that there was a war on, I agreed
To join this new crusade; the Golden Calf

Mooed once and Pegasus whinnied. 'There will be need
For the moment of course,' said Harrap, 'for much work
Of a purely ephemeral kind; you will have to feed

The tall transmitters with hot news – Dunkirk,
Tobruk or Singapore, you will have to set
Traps for your neutral listeners, Yank or Turk,

While your blacked-out compatriots must be met
Half way – half reprimanded and half flattered,
Cajoled to half remember and half forget;

For that is propaganda. Bored and battered
And sleeping in long tubes like suspect germs
They must be told that what they once thought mattered

Still matters. It is not much; but Goebbels' terms
Of reference are worse. The time is ripe
For lame dogs jumping stiles and turning worms.'

Harrap ended; Herriot filled his pipe
(Who was going to be my boss) and Devlin, who
Was going to be my colleague, took his swipe

At both their dignities, the evening grew
Significant and inconsequent. Content
To find there was ephemeral work to do,

Ephemeral work I did. The skies were rent
And I took notes; delicate whippets of fire
Hurdled the streets, the cockney firmament

Ran with flamingoes' blood and Dido's pyre
Burnt high and wide and randy over the Thames
While a mixed metaphor of high-tension wire

Capsized, still clutching heaven by the hems
And ripping off a star. Devlin and I
Fished in this troubled air, our stratagems

Landed some strange old boots and other curious fry;
Thus in a concrete tank of formaldehyde
Beneath one bombed museum I cast a fly

And up there rose to take it, side by side
Bobbing and churning in the purple wave,
His stomach stripped for the scalpel, London's pride

Of late, the giant panda, and with grave
Eyes neatly closed and small wrists neatly crossed
The one exhibit the rescue squad could save

Of Hunter's own, who with such care and cost
Began this whole collection, an unborn
But eighteenth-century baby, groomed and glossed

Like a small soapstone Buddha, his clouts unworn
But hooded in half his cowl. I threw him back
In his tank; he seemed too odd a fish to adorn

A twentieth-century war. We changed our tack
And jinked through gutted shop and staring church
Prospecting for more relevant bric-à-brac,

Copy and yet more copy. Such research
Was much preformulated, yet we found
Some facts that left our blueprints in the lurch,

Some lines not broad enough nor numbers round
Enough to be scored on the slate or paid in the lump;
Maybe our formulae were not so sound,

Our big slick words due for the rubbish dump,
Maybe ideals were less than men; maybe
The pen was weaker than the stirrup pump.

Devlin and I continued; what we see
Is sometimes more than what we think we feel.
Our sights unfelt ourselves. In some degree

[125]

What mind has passed sheer stocks and stones repeal,
And both self-pity and self-conceit give way
To a pride that sprouts from stocks or stones or steel.

Thus humbled and exalted day by day
We scratched among the debris. The war flowed by
In short or medium waves with a disarray

Of initials, M.I.5, O.W.I.,
Of names, Metaxas or Mihailovitch,
Of doubts and queries, If and But and Why,

Provided and Supposing, Where and Which,
And most especially When: oh when would this
Thing start or that thing stop? We were always rich

In speculation, poor in synthesis,
But at last the whole thing stopped, the war was over,
And each prognostication of blight or bliss

Immediately out of date, the cliffs of Dover
Once more mere cliffs. As usual, Devlin sang
Folksongs, the Farmer's Boy and the Bold Drover

And the Foggy Dew, but they had lost their tang
Not being heard in danger, the sunset-tinted
Balloons were down, firemen's and airmen's slang

Like the Four Freedoms and other newly minted
Phrases would soon be obsolete and the wire
Stripped from the bathing beach and the blueprints
                                              unprinted

And democracy undressed. 'If you so desire,'
My employers said, 'this office will now return
To a peacetime footing where we might require

Your further service.' I could not discern
Much choice; it might in fact be better to give
Such service, better to bury than to burn.

I stayed. On my peacetime feet. There was little alternative.

from A Hand of Snapshots

The Left-Behind

Peering into your stout you see a past of lazybeds,
A liner moving west, leaving the husk of home,
Its white wake lashing round your pimpled haycocks.
Drink up, Rip MacWinkle. The night is old.

Where can you find a fire that burns and gives no warmth?
Where is the tall ship that chose to run on a rock?
Where are there more fish than ever filled the ocean?
Where can you find a clock that strikes when it has stopped?

Oh, poverty is the fire that burns and gives no warmth.
My youth is the tall ship that chose to run on a rock.
Men yet unborn could more than fill the ocean,
And death is the black clock that strikes when it has
                                                    stopped.

The Once-in-Passing

And here the cross on the window means myself
But that window does not open;
Born here, I should have proved a different self.
Such vistas dare not open;
For what can walk or talk without tongue or feet?

Here for a month to spend but not to earn,
How could I even imagine
Such a life here that my plain days could earn
The life my dreams imagine?
For what takes root or grows that owns no root?

Yet here for a month, and for this once in passing,
I can imagine at least
The permanence of what passes,
As though the window opened
And the ancient cross on the hillside meant myself.

Nature Notes

Dandelions

Incorrigible, brash,
They brightened the cinder path of my childhood,
Unsubtle, the opposite of primroses,
But, unlike primroses, capable
Of growing anywhere, railway track, pierhead,
Like our extrovert friends who never
Make us fall in love, yet fill
The primroseless roseless gaps.

Cats

Incorrigible, uncommitted,
They leavened the long flat hours of my childhood,
Subtle, the opposite of dogs,
And, unlike dogs, capable
Of flirting, falling, and yawning anywhere,
Like women who want no contract
But going their own way
Make the way of their lovers lighter.

Corncrakes

Incorrigible, unmusical,
They bridged the surrounding hedge of my childhood,
Unsubtle, the opposite of blackbirds,
But, unlike blackbirds, capable
Anywhere they are of endorsing summer
Like loud men around the corner
Whom we never see but whose raucous
Voices can give us confidence.

The Sea

Incorrigible, ruthless,
It rattled the shingly beach of my childhood,
Subtle, the opposite of earth,
And, unlike earth, capable
Any time at all of proclaiming eternity
Like something or someone to whom
We have to surrender, finding
Through that surrender life.

Reflections

The mirror above my fireplace reflects the reflected
Room in my window; I look in the mirror at night
And see two rooms, the first where left is right
And the second, beyond the reflected window, corrected
But there I am standing back to my back. The standard
Lamp comes thrice in my mirror, twice in my window,
The fire in the mirror lies two rooms away through the
                                                    window,
The fire in the window lies one room away down the
                                                    terrace,
My actual room stands sandwiched between confections
Of night and lights and glass and in both directions
I can see beyond and through the reflections the street
                                                    lamps
At home outdoors where my indoors rooms lie stranded,
Where a taxi perhaps will drive in through the bookcase
Whose books are not for reading and past the fire
Which gives no warmth and pull up by my desk
At which I cannot write since I am not lefthanded.

Hold-up

The lights were red, refused to change,
Ash-ends grew longer, no one spoke,
The papers faded in their hands,
The bubbles in the football pools
Went flat, the hot news froze, the dates
They could not keep were dropped like charred
Matches, the girls no longer flagged
Their sex, besides the code was lost,
The engine stalled, a tall glass box
On the pavement held a corpse in pickle
His ear still cocked, and no one spoke,
No number rang, for miles behind
The other buses nudged and blared
And no one dared get out. The conductress
Was dark and lost, refused to change.

The Truisms

His father gave him a box of truisms
Shaped like a coffin, then his father died;
The truisms remained on the mantelpiece
As wooden as the playbox they had been packed in
Or that other his father skulked inside.

Then he left home, left the truisms behind him
Still on the mantelpiece, met love, met war,
Sordor, disappointment, defeat, betrayal,
Till through disbeliefs he arrived at a house
He could not remember seeing before,

And he walked straight in; it was where he had come from
And something told him the way to behave.
He raised his hand and blessed his home;
The truisms flew and perched on his shoulders
And a tall tree sprouted from his father's grave.

The Blasphemies

The sin against the Holy . . . though what
He wondered was it? Cold in his bed
He thought: If I think those words I know
Yet must not be thinking – Come to the hurdle
And I shall be damned through thinking Damn –
But Whom? But no! Those words are unthinkable;
Damn anyone else, but once I – No,
Here lies the unforgivable blasphemy.
So pulling the cold sheets over his head
He swore to himself he had not thought
Those words he knew but never admitted.
To be damned at seven years old was early.

[133]

Ten years later, his Who's Who
No longer cosmic, he turned to parody –
Prayers, hymns, the Apostles' Creed –
Preening himself as a gay blasphemer,
But what is a practical joke in a world
Of nonsense, what is a rational attitude
Towards politics in a world of ciphers,
Towards sex if you lack all lust, towards art
If you do not believe in communication?
And what is a joke about God if you do not
Accept His existence? Where is the blasphemy?
No Hell at seventeen feels empty.

Rising thirty, he had decided
God was a mere expletive, a cheap one,
No longer worth a laugh, no longer
A proper occasion to prove one's freedom
By denying something not worth denying.
So humanism was all and the only
Sin was the sin against the Human –
But you could not call it Ghost for that
Was merely emotive; the only – you could not
Call it sin for that was emotive –
The only failure was not to face
The facts. But at thirty what are the facts?

Ten years later, in need of myth,
He thought: I can use my childhood symbols
Divorced from their context, Manger and Cross
Could do very well for Tom Dick and Harry –
Have we not all of us been in a war
So have we not carried call it a cross
Which was never our fault? Yet how can a cross
Be never your fault? The words of the myth,
Now merely that and no longer faith,
Melt in his hands which were never proved
Hard as nails, nor can he longer
Speak for the world – or himself – at forty.

Forty to fifty. In ten years
He grew to feel the issue irrelevant:
Tom Dick and Harry were not Christ
And whether Christ were God or not
And whether there were a God or not
The word was inadequate. For himself
He was not Tom or Dick or Harry,
Let alone God, he was merely fifty,
No one and nowhere else, a walking
Question but no more cheap than any
Question or quest is cheap. The sin
Against the Holy Ghost – What is it?

Bad Dream

The window was made of ice with bears lumbering across
it,
Bears the size of flies;
The ceiling was one great web with flies cantankering in it,
Flies the size of men;
The floor was riddled with holes with men phutscuttering
down them
Into the jaws of mice.

Outside there were no other houses, only bedizened
hoardings
With panties prancing on them
And an endless file of chromium-plated lamp posts
With corpses dangling from them
And one gaunt ruined church with a burglar alarm
filibustering
High and dry in the steeple.

Here then the young man came who wanted to eat and
drink,
To play, pray, make love;
Electronic voices nagged at him out of the filtered air,
The eyes on the hoarding winked;
He knocked at the door of the house, the bears buzzed and
the flies
Howled to him to come in.

Inside he found a table laid for two, a mirror
Flanking the double bed,

On the night table a scent spray, a tin of biscuits, a bible,
   A crucifix on the wall
And beside it a comic postcard: all this he carefully noticed
   And then he noticed the floor

Bomb-pocked with tiny holes, from one of which there
                                                    rose
   One tiny wisp of white.
He watched as it clawed the air two inches from the floor
   And saw it for what it was,
The arm of a girl, he watched and just could hear her voice
   Say: Wait! Wait till I grow.

And the arm grew and he wished to bend and clutch the
                                                    hand
   But found he could no more move,
The arm grew and the fingers groped for help, the voice
   That had grown with the arm, the voice
That was now a woman's about to be saved or lost was
                                                    calling
   For help. He could not move.

Then everything buzzed and boomed. The chaps outside
                              on the lamp posts
   Hooted, broke wind, and wept,
Men the size of flies dropped down his neck while the
                                                    mansized
   Flies gave just three cheers
And he could not move. The darkness under the floor gave
                                                    just
   One shriek. The arm was gone.

Soap Suds

This brand of soap has the same smell as once in the big
House he visited when he was eight: the walls of the
                                        bathroom open
To reveal a lawn where a great yellow ball rolls back
                                        through a hoop
To rest at the head of a mallet held in the hands of a child.

And these were the joys of that house: a tower with a
                                        telescope;
Two great faded globes, one of the earth, one of the stars;
A stuffed black dog in the hall; a walled garden with bees;
A rabbit warren; a rockery; a vine under glass; the sea.

To which he has now returned. The day of course is fine
And a grown-up voice cries Play! The mallet slowly swings,
Then crack, a great gong booms from the dog-dark hall and
                                        the ball
Skims forward through the hoop and then through the
                                        next and then

Through hoops where no hoops were and each dissolves
                                        in turn
And the grass has grown head-high and an angry voice
                                        cries Play!
But the ball is lost and the mallet slipped long since from
                                        the hands
Under the running tap that are not the hands of a child.

The Suicide

And this, ladies and gentlemen, whom I am not in fact
Conducting, was his office all those minutes ago,
This man you never heard of. There are the bills
In the intray, the ash in the ashtray, the grey memoranda
                                stacked

Against him, the serried ranks of the box-files, the packed
Jury of his unanswered correspondence
Nodding under the paperweight in the breeze
From the window by which he left; and here is the cracked
Receiver that never got mended and here is the jotter
With his last doodle which might be his own digestive tract
Ulcer and all or might be the flowery maze
Through which he had wandered deliciously till he
                                stumbled

Suddenly finally conscious of all he lacked
On a manhole under the hollyhocks. The pencil
Point had obviously broken, yet, when he left this room
By catdrop sleight-of-foot or simple vanishing act,
To those who knew him for all that mess in the street
This man with the shy smile has left behind
Something that was intact.

The Taxis

In the first taxi he was alone tra-la,
No extras on the clock. He tipped ninepence
But the cabby, while he thanked him, looked askance
As though to suggest someone had bummed a ride.

In the second taxi he was alone tra-la
But the clock showed sixpence extra; he tipped according
And the cabby from out his muffler said: 'Make sure
You have left nothing behind tra-la between you.'

In the third taxi he was alone tra-la
But the tip-up seats were down and there was an extra
Charge of one-and-sixpence and an odd
Scent that reminded him of a trip to Cannes.

As for the fourth taxi, he was alone
Tra-la when he hailed it but the cabby looked
Through him and said: 'I can't tra-la well take
So many people, not to speak of the dog.'

Charon

The conductor's hands were black with money:
Hold on to your ticket, he said, the inspector's
Mind is black with suspicion, and hold on to
That dissolving map. We moved through London,
We could see the pigeons through the glass but failed
To hear their rumours of wars, we could see
The lost dog barking but never knew
That his bark was as shrill as a cock crowing,
We just jogged on, at each request
Stop there was a crowd of aggressively vacant
Faces, we just jogged on, eternity
Gave itself airs in revolving lights
And then we came to the Thames and all
The bridges were down, the further shore
Was lost in fog, so we asked the conductor
What we should do. He said: Take the ferry
Faute de mieux. We flicked the flashlight
And there was the ferryman just as Virgil
And Dante had seen him. He looked at us coldly
And his eyes were dead and his hands on the oar
Were black with obols and varicose veins
Marbled his calves and he said to us coldly:
If you want to die you will have to pay for it.

The Introduction

They were introduced in a grave glade
And she frightened him because she was young
And thus too late. Crawly crawly
Went the twigs above their heads and beneath
The grass beneath their feet the larvae
Split themselves laughing. Crawly crawly
Went the cloud above the treetops reaching
For a sun that lacked the nerve to set
And he frightened her because he was old
And thus too early. Crawly crawly
Went the string quartet that was tuning up
In the back of the mind. You two should have met
Long since, he said, or else not now.
The string quartet in the back of the mind
Was all tuned up with nowhere to go.
They were introduced in a green grave.

Tree Party

Your health, Master Willow. Contrive me a bat
To strike a red ball; apart from that
In the last resort I must hang my harp on you.

Your health, Master Oak. You emblem of strength,
Why must your doings be done at such length?
Beware lest the ironclad ages catch up with you.

[142]

Your health, Master Blackthorn. Be live and be quick,
Provide the black priest with a big black stick
That his ignorant flock may go straight for the fear of you.

Your health, Master Palm. If you brew us some toddy
To deliver us out of by means of the body,
We will burn all our bridges and rickshaws in praise of you.

Your health, Master Pine. Though sailing be past
Let you fly your own colours upon your own mast
And rig us a crow's nest to keep a look out from you.

Your health, Master Elm. Of giants arboreal
Poets have found you the most immemorial
And yet the big winds may discover the fault in you.

Your health, Master Hazel. On Hallow-e'en
Your nuts are to gather but not to be seen
Are the twittering ghosts that perforce are alive in you.

Your health, Master Holly. Of all the trees
That decorate parlour walls you please
Yet who would have thought you had so much blood in you?

Your health, Master Apple. Your topmost bough
Entices us to come climbing now
For all that old rumour there might be a snake in you.

Your health, Master Redwood. The record is yours
For the girth that astounds, the sap that endures,
But where are the creatures that once came to nest in you?

Your health, Master Banyan, but do not get drunk
Or you may not distinguish your limbs from your trunk
And the sense of Above and Below will be lost on you.

Your health, Master Bo-Tree. If Buddha should come
Yet again, yet again make your branches keep mum
That his words yet again may drop honey by leave of you.

Your health, Master Yew. My bones are few
And I fully admit my rent is due,
But do not be vexed, I will postdate a cheque for you.

Coda

Maybe we knew each other better
When the night was young and unrepeated
And the moon stood still over Jericho.

So much for the past; in the present
There are moments caught between heart-beats
When maybe we know each other better.

But what is that clinking in the darkness?
Maybe we shall know each other better
When the tunnels meet beneath the mountain.

THOMAS KINSELLA   1928–

In the Ringwood

As I roved out impatiently
Good Friday with my bride
To drink in the rivered Ringwood
The draughty season's pride
A fell dismay held suddenly
Our feet on the green hill-side.

The yellow Spring on Vinegar Hill,
The smile of Slaney water,
The wind that swept the Ringwood,
Grew dark with ancient slaughter.
My love cried out and I beheld her
Change to Sorrow's daughter.

'Ravenhair, what rending
Set those red lips a-shriek,
And dealt those locks in black lament
Like blows on your white cheek,
That in your looks outlandishly
Both woe and fury speak?'

As sharp a lance as the fatal heron
There on the sunken tree
Will strike in the stones of the river
Was the gaze she bent on me.
O her robe into her right hand
She gathered grievously.

'Many times the civil lover
Climbed that pleasant place,
Many times despairing
Died in his love's face,
His spittle turned to vinegar,
Blood in his embrace.

Love that is every miracle
Is torn apart and rent.
The human turns awry
The poles of the firmament.
The fish's bright side is pierced
And good again is spent.

Though every stem on Vinegar Hill
And stone on the Slaney's bed
And every leaf in the living Ringwood
Builds till it is dead
Yet heart and hand, accomplished,
Destroy until they dread.

Dread, a grey devourer,
Stalks in the shade of love.
The dark that dogs our feet
Eats what is sickened of.
The End that stalks Beginning
Hurries home its drove.'

I kissed three times her shivering lips.
I drank their naked chill.
I watched the river shining
Where the heron wiped his bill.
I took my love in my icy arms
In the Spring on Ringwood Hill.

Another September

Dreams fled away, this country bedroom, raw
With the touch of the dawn, wrapped in a minor peace,
Hears through an open window the garden draw
Long pitch black breaths, lay bare its apple trees,
Ripe pear trees, brambles, windfall-sweetened soil,
Exhale rough sweetness against the starry slates.
Nearer the river sleeps St John's, all toil
Locked fast inside a dream with iron gates.

Domestic Autumn, like an animal
Long used to handling by those countrymen,
Rubs her kind hide against the bedroom wall
Sensing a fragrant child come back again
– Not this half-tolerated consciousness,
Its own cold season never done,
But that unspeaking daughter, growing less
Familiar where we fell asleep as one.

Wakeful moth-wings blunder near a chair,
Toss their light shell at the glass, and go
To inhabit the living starlight. Stranded hair
Stirs on the still linen. It is as though
The black breathing that billows her sleep, her name,
Drugged under judgment, waned and – bearing daggers
And balances – down the lampless darkness they came,
Moving like women: Justice, Truth, such figures.

Baggot Street Deserta

Lulled, at silence, the spent attack.
The will to work is laid aside.
The breaking-cry, the strain of the rack,
Yield, are at peace. The window is wide
On a crawling arch of stars, and the night
Reacts faintly to the mathematic
Passion of a cello suite
Plotting the quiet of my attic.
A mile away the river toils
Its buttressed fathoms out to sea;
Tucked in the mountains, many miles
Away from its roaring outcome, a shy
Gasp of waters in the gorse
Is sonneting origins. Dreamers' heads
Lie mesmerized in Dublin's beds
Flashing with images, Adam's morse.

A cigarette, the moon, a sigh
Of educated boredom, greet
A curlew's lingering threadbare cry
Of common loss. Compassionate,
I add my call of exile, half-
Buried longing, half-serious
Anger and the rueful laugh.
We fly into our risk, the spurious.

Versing, like an exile, makes
A virtuoso of the heart,
Interpreting the old mistakes
And discords in a work of Art
For the One, a private masterpiece
Of doctored recollections. Truth
Concedes, before the dew, its place
In the spray of dried forgettings Youth
Collected when they were a single
Furious undissected bloom.
A voice clarifies when the tingle
Dies out of the nerves of time:
Endure and let the present punish.
Looking backward, all is lost;
The Past becomes a fairy bog
Alive with fancies, double crossed
By pad of owl and hoot of dog,
Where shaven, serious-minded men
Appear with lucid theses, after
Which they don the mists again
With trackless, cotton-silly laughter;

Secretly a swollen Burke
Assists a decomposing Hare
To cart a body of good work
With midnight mutterings off somewhere;
The goddess who had light for thighs
Grows feet of dung and takes to bed,
Affronting horror-stricken eyes,
The marsh bird that children dread.

I nonetheless inflict, endure,
Tedium, intracordal hurt,
The sting of memory's quick, the drear
Uprooting, burying, prising apart
Of loves a strident adolescent
Spent in doubt and vanity.
All feed a single stream, impassioned
Now with obsessed honesty,
A tugging scruple that can keep
Clear eyes staring down the mile,
The thousand fathoms, into sleep.
Fingers cold against the sill
Feel, below the stress of flight,
The slow implosion of my pulse
In a wrist with poet's cramp, a tight
Beat tapping out endless calls
Into the dark, as the alien
Garrison in my own blood
Keeps constant contact with the main
Mystery, not to be understood.
Out where imagination arches
Chilly points of light transact
The business of the border-marches

Of the Real, and I – a fact
That may be countered or may not –
Find their privacy complete.

My quarter-inch of cigarette
Goes flaring down to Baggot Street.

Love

Sisters

Grim Deirdre sought the stony fist, her grief
Capped at last by insult. Pierce's bride,
Sybil Ferriter, fluttered like a leaf
And fell in courtly love to stain the tide.
Each for a murdered husband – hanged in silk
Or speared in harness – threw her body wide,
And offered treachery a bloody milk;
Each cast the other's shadow when she died.

A Garden on the Point

Now it is Easter and the speckled bean
Breaks open underground, the liquid snail
Winces and waits, trapped on the lawn's light green;
The burdened clothes-line heaves and barks in the gale,
And lost in flowers near the garage wall
Child and mother fumble, tidy, restrain.

And now great ebb tides lift to the light of day
The sea-bed's briny chambers of decay.

Song

Handclasp at Euston

The engine screams and Murphy, isolate
– Chalk-white, comedian – in the smoky glare,
Dwindles among the churns and tenders. Weight,
Person, race, the human, dwindle there.
I bow to the cases cluttering the rack,
Their handles black with sweat of exile. Wales,
Wave and home; I close my eyes. The track
Swerves to a greener world: sea-rock, thigh-scales.

At the Heart

Heraldic, hatched in gold, a sacred tree
Stands absorbed, tinkering with the slight
Thrumming of birds, the flicker of energy
Thrown and caught, the blows and burdens of flight.
Roots deepen; disciplines proliferate
And wings more fragile are brought into play.
Timber matures, the game grows nobler, yet
Not one has sped direct as appetite.

Fire and Ice

Two creatures face each other, fixed in song,
Satyr and nymph, across the darkening brain.
I dream of reason and the first grows strong,
Drunk as a whirlwind on the sweating grain;
I dream of drunkenness and, freed from strain,
The second murmurs like a fingered gong;
I sink beneath the dream: his words grow sane,
Her pupils glow with pleasure all night long.

[154]

Downstream

Drifting to meet us on the darkening stage
A pattern shivered; whorling in its place
Another held us in a living cage
Then broke to its reordered phase of grace.

Again in the mirrored dusk the paddles sank.
  We thrust forward, swaying both as one.
  The ripples widened to the ghostly bank

Where willows, with their shadows half undone,
  Hung to the water, mowing like the blind.
  The current seized our skiff. We let it run

Grazing the reeds, and let the land unwind
  In stealth on either hand. Dark woods: a door
  Opened and shut. The clear sky fell behind,

The channel shrank. Thick slopes from shore to shore
  Lowered a matted arch. I thought of roots
  Crawling full of pike on the river-floor

To cage us in, sensed the furred night-brutes
  Halt in their trails, twitching their tiny brushes.
  What plopped in the reeds and stirred between the
                                                    shoots?

Then I remembered how among those bushes
  A man one night fell sick and left his shell
  Collapsed, half eaten, like a rotted thrush's

To frighten stumbling children. 'You could tell',
   My co-shadow murmured, 'by the hands
   He died in terror.' And the cold of hell,

Like mortal jaws, the alleys of the wood
   Fell-to behind us. At its heart, a ghost
   Glimmered briefly with my gift of blood

– Spreadeagled on a rack of leaves, almost
   Remembering. It looked full at the sky,
   Calmly encountering the starry host,

Meeting their silver eyes with silver eye.
   An X of wavering flesh, a skull of light,
   Extinguished in our wake without a sigh.

Then the current shuddered in its flight
   And swerved on pliant muscle; we were sped
   Through sudden peace into a pit of night:

The Mill-Hole, whose rocky fathoms fed
   On moss and pure depth and the cold fin
   Turning in its heart. The river bed

Called to our flesh. Across the watery skin,
   Breathless, our shell trembled. The abyss . . .
   We shipped our oars in dread. Now, deeper in,

Something shifted in sleep, a quiet hiss
   As we slipped by. Adrift . . . A milk-white breast . . .
   A shuffle of wings betrayed with a feathery kiss

[156]

A soul of white with darkness for a nest.
  The creature bore the night so tranquilly
  I lifted up my eyes. There without rest

A limb-lightness, a terror in the glands,
  Pierced again as when that story first
  Froze my blood: the soil of other lands

Drank lives that summer with a body thirst;
  Nerveless by the European pit
  – Ourselves through seven hundred years accurst –

We saw the barren world obscurely lit
  By tall chimneys flickering in their pall,
  The haunt of swinish man – each day a spit

That, turning, sweated war, each night a fall
  Back to the evil dream where rodents ply,
  Man-rumped, sow-headed, busy with whip and maul

Among nude herds of the damned. It seemed that I,
  Coming to conscience on that lip of dread,
  Still dreamed, impervious to calamity,

Imagining a formal drift of the dead
  Stretched calm as effigies on velvet dust,
  Scattered on starlit slopes with arms outspread

And eyes of silver – when that story thrust
  Pungent horror and an actual mess
  Into my very face, and taste I must.

Then hungry joy and sickening distress
   Fumbled together by the brimming flood,
   And night consumed a hopeless loneliness.

The phantoms of the overhanging sky
   Occupied their stations and descended;
   Another moment, to the starlit eye,

The slow, downstreaming dead, it seemed, were blended
   One with those silver hordes, and briefly shared
   Their order, glittering. And then impended

A barrier of rock that turned and bared
   A varied barrenness as toward its base
   We glided – blotting heaven as it towered –

Searching the darkness for a landing place.

Mirror in February

   The day dawns with scent of must and rain,
   Of opened soil, dark trees, dry bedroom air.
   Under the fading lamp, half dressed – my brain
   Idling on some compulsive fantasy –
   I towel my shaven lip and stop, and stare,
   Riveted by a dark exhausted eye,
   A dry downturning mouth.

It seems again that it is time to learn,
In this untiring, crumbling place of growth
To which, for the time being, I return.
Now plainly in the mirror of my soul
I read that I have looked my last on youth
And little more; for they are not made whole
That reach the age of Christ.

Below my window the awakening trees,
Hacked clean for better bearing, stand defaced
Suffering their brute necessities,
And how should the flesh not quail that span for span
Is mutilated more? In slow distaste
I fold my towel with what grace I can,
Not young and not renewable, but man.

Wormwood

I have dreamt it again: standing suddenly still
In a thicket, among wet trees, stunned, minutely
Shuddering, hearing a wooden echo escape.

A mossy floor, almost colourless, disappears
In depths of rain among the tree shapes.
I am straining, tasting that echo a second longer.

If I can hold it . . . familiar if I can hold it . . .
A black tree with a double trunk – two trees
Grown into one – throws up its blurred branches.

[159]

The two trunks in their infinitesimal dance of growth
Have turned completely about one another, their join
A slowly twisted scar, that I recognize . . .

A quick arc flashes sidewise in the air,
A heavy blade in flight. A wooden stroke:
Iron sinks in the gasping core.

                              I will dream it again.

Ballydavid Pier

Noon. The luminous tide
Climbs through the heat, covering
Grey shingle. A film of scum
Searches first among litter,
Cloudy with (I remember)
Life; then crystal-clear shallows
Cool on the stones, silent
With shells and claws, white fish bones;
Farther out a bag of flesh,
Foetus of goat or sheep
Wavers below the surface.

Allegory forms of itself:
The line of life creeps upward
Replacing one world with another,
The welter of its advance
Sinks down into clarity,
Slowly the more foul
Monsters of loss digest . . .

Small monster of true flesh
Brought forth somewhere
In bloody confusion and error
And flung into bitterness,
Blood washed white:
Does that structure satisfy?

The ghost tissue hangs unresisting
In allegorical waters,
Lost in self-search
– A swollen blind brow
Humbly crumpled over
Budding limbs, unshaken
By the spasms of birth or death.

The Angelus. Faint bell-notes
From some church in the distance
Tremble over the water.
It is nothing. The vacant harbour
Is filling; it will empty.
The misbirth touches the surface
And glistens like quicksilver.

Leaf-eater

On a shrub in the heart of the garden,
On an outer leaf, a grub twists
Half its body, a tendril,
This way and that in blind
Space: no leaf or twig
Anywhere in reach; then gropes
Back on itself and begins
To eat its own leaf.

Ancestor

I was going up to say something,
and stopped. Her profile against the curtains
was old, and dark like a hunting bird's.

It was the way she perched on the high stool,
staring into herself, with one fist
gripping the side of the barrier around her desk
– or her head held by something, from inside.
And not caring for anything around her
or anyone there by the shelves.
I caught a faint smell, musky and queer.

I may have made some sound – she stopped rocking
and pressed her fist in her lap; then she stood up
and shut down the lid of the desk, and turned the key.
She shoved a small bottle under her aprons
and came toward me, darkening the passageway.

Ancestor . . . among sweet- and fruit-boxes.
Her black heart . . .
                    Was that a sigh?
– brushing by me in the shadows,
with her heaped aprons, through the red hangings
to the scullery, and down to the back room.

Touching the River

That nude kneeling so sad-seeming
on her shelf of moss, how timelessly
– all sepia – her arm reaches down
to let her fingers, affectedly trailing,
stick in the stopped brown water.

Rivery movement; gurgling, clay-fresh;
light murmuring over the surface;
bubbling . . .
                Our unstopped
flesh and senses – how they vanish!

Though we kneel on the brink and drive our stare
down – *now* – into the current.
Though everywhere in the wet fields – listen –
the reeds are shivering (one clump of them
nestling a lark's eggs, I know, in a hoof-print).

His Father's Hands

I drank firmly
and set the glass down between us firmly.
You were saying.

My father.
Was saying.

His finger prodded and prodded,
marring his point. Emphas-
emphasemphasis.

I have watched
his father's hands before him

   cupped, and tightening the black Plug
between knife and thumb,
carving off little curlicues
to rub them in the dark of his palms,

or cutting into new leather at his bench,
levering a groove open with his thumb,
insinuating wet sprigs for the hammer.

He kept the sprigs in mouthfuls
and brought them out in silvery
units between his lips.

I took a pinch out of their hole
and knocked them one by one into the wood,
bright points among hundreds gone black,
other children's – cousins and others, grown up.

   Or his bow hand scarcely moving,
scraping in the dark corners near the fire,
his plump fingers shifting on the strings.

To his deaf, inclined head
he hugged the fiddle's body,
whispering with the tune

with breaking heart
whene'er I hear
in privacy, across a blocked void,

the wind that shakes the barley.
The wind . . .
round her grave . . .

on my breast in blood she died . . .
But blood for blood without remorse
I've ta'en . . .

Beyond that.

*

Your family, Thomas, met with and helped
many of the Croppies in hiding from the Yeos
or on their way home after the defeat
in south Wexford. They sheltered the Laceys
who were later hanged on the Bridge in Ballinglen
between Tinahely and Anacorra.

From hearsay, as far as I can tell
the Men Folk were either Stone Cutters
or masons or probably both.
                              In the 18
and late 1700s even the farmers
had some other trade to make a living.

They lived in Farnese among a Colony
of North of Ireland or Scotch settlers left there
in some of the dispersals or migrations
which occurred in this Area of Wicklow and Wexford
and Carlow. And some years before that time
the Family came from somewhere around Tullow.

Beyond that.

*

Littered uplands. Dense grass. Rocks everywhere,
wet underneath, retaining memory of the long cold.

First, a prow of land
chosen, and webbed with tracks;
then boulders chosen
and sloped together, stabilized in menace.

I do not like this place.
I do not think the people who lived here
were ever happy. It feels evil.
Terrible things happened.
I feel afraid here when I am on my own.

*

Dispersals or migrations.
Through what evolutions or accidents
toward that peace and patience
by the fireside, that blocked gentleness . . .

That serene pause, with the slashing knife,
in kindly mockery,
as I busy myself with my little nails
at the rude block, his bench.

The blood advancing
– gorging vessel after vessel –
and altering in them
one by one.

Behold, that gentleness already
modulated twice, in others:
to earnestness and iteration;
to an offhandedness, repressing various impulses.

*

Extraordinary . . . The big block – I found it
years afterward in a corner of the yard
in sunlight after rain
and stood it up, wet and black:
it turned under my hands, an axis
of light flashing down its length,
and the wood's soft flesh broke open,
countless little nails
squirming and dropping out of it.

Tao and Unfitness at Inistiogue
on the River Nore

Noon

The black flies kept nagging in the heat.
Swarms of them, at every step, snarled
off pats of cow dung spattered in the grass.

Move, if you move, like water.

The punts were knocking by the boathouse, at full tide.
Volumes of water turned the river curve
hushed under an insect haze.

                  Slips of white,
trout bellies, flicked in the corner of the eye
and dropped back onto the deep mirror.

Respond. Do not interfere. Echo.

Thick green woods along the opposite bank
climbed up from a root-dark recess
eaved with mud-whitened leaves.

*

In a matter of hours all that water is gone,
except for a channel near the far side.
Muck and shingle and pools where the children
wade, stabbing flatfish.

Afternoon

Inistiogue itself is perfectly lovely,
like a typical English village, but a bit sullen.
Our voices echoed in sunny corners
among the old houses; we admired
the stonework and gateways, the interplay
of roofs and angled streets.

The square, with its 'village green', lay empty.
The little shops had hardly anything.
The Protestant church was guarded by a woman
of about forty, a retainer, spastic
and indistinct, who drove us out.

An obelisk to the Brownsfoords and a Victorian
Celto-Gothic drinking fountain, erected
by a Tighe widow for the villagers,
'erected' in the centre. An astronomical-looking
sundial stood sentry on a platform
on the corner where High Street went up out of the square.

We drove up, past a long-handled water pump
placed at the turn, with an eye to the effect,
then out of the town for a quarter of a mile
above the valley, and came to the dead gate
of Woodstock, once home of the Tighes.

*

The great ruin presented its flat front
at us, sunstruck. The children disappeared.
Eleanor picked her way around a big fallen branch
and away along the face toward the outbuildings.
I took the grassy front steps and was gathered up
in a brick-red stillness. A rook clattered out of the dining
room.

A sapling, hooked thirty feet up
in a cracked corner, held out a ghost-green
cirrus of leaves. Cavities
of collapsed fireplaces connected silently
about the walls. Deserted spaces, complicated
by door-openings everywhere.

There was a path up among bushes and nettles
over the beaten debris, then a drop, where bricks
and plaster and rafters had fallen into the kitchens.
A line of small choked arches . . . The pantries, possibly.

Be still, as though pure.

A brick, and its dust, fell.

Nightfall

The trees we drove under in the dusk
as we threaded back along the river through the woods
were no mere dark growth, but a flitting-place
for ragged feeling, old angers and rumours . . .

Black and Tan ghosts up there, at home
on the Woodstock heights: an iron mouth
scanning the Kilkenny road: the house
gutted by the townspeople and burned to ruins . . .

The little Ford we met, and inched past, full of men
we had noticed along the river bank during the week,
disappeared behind us into a fifty-year-old night.
Even their caps and raincoats . . .

Sons, or grandsons. Poachers.
                              Mud-tasted salmon
slithering in a plastic bag around the boot,
bloodied muscles, disputed since King John.

The ghosts of daughters of the family
waited in the uncut grass as we drove
down to our mock-Austrian lodge and stopped.

*

We untied the punt in the half-light, and pushed out
to take a last hour on the river, until night.
We drifted, but stayed almost still.
The current underneath us
and the tide coming back to the full
cancelled in a gleaming calm, punctuated
by the plop of fish.

Down on the water . . . at eye level . . . in the little light
remaining overhead . . . the mayfly passed in a loose drift,
thick and frail, a hatch slow with sex,
separate morsels trailing their slack filaments,
olive, pale evening dun, imagoes, unseen eggs
dropping from the air, subimagoes, the river filled
with their nymphs ascending and excited trout.

Be subtle, as though not there.

We were near the island – no more than a dark mass
on a sheet of silver – when a man appeared in midriver
quickly and with scarcely a sound, his paddle touching
left and right of the prow, with a sack behind him.
The flat cot's long body slid past effortless
as a fish, sinewing from side to side,
as he passed us and vanished.

JOHN MONTAGUE   1929–

Soliloquy on a Southern Strand

A priest, holidaying on the coast
outside Sydney, thinks nostalgically
of his boyhood in Ireland

When I was young, it was much simpler;
I saw God standing on a local hill,
His eyes were gentle and soft birds
Sang in chorus to his voice until
My body trembled, ardent in submission.
The friar came to preach the yearly sermon
For Retreat, and cried among the flaring candles:
'O children, children, if you but knew,
'Each hair is counted, everything you do
'Offends or sweetens His five wounds!'
A priest with a harsh and tuneless voice,
Raising his brown-robed arms to cry:
'Like this candle-end, the body gutters out to die!'
Calling us all to do penance and rejoice.

Hearing the preacher speak, I knew my mind
And wished to serve, leaving the friendly farm
For years of college. At first I found it strange
And feared the boys with smoother hands and voices:
I lay awake at night, longed for home.
I heard the town boys laughing in the dark
At things that made me burn with shame,
And where the votive candles whispered into wax
Hesitantly I spoke my treasured doubts,
Conquering all my passions in your Name.

[175]

I weathered years of sameness
Until I stood before the Cathedral altar,
A burly country boy but new-made priest;
My mother watched in happiness and peace.

The young people crowd the shore now,
Rushing from Sydney, like lemmings, to the sea.
Heat plays upon the glaring cluttered beach,
Casts as in a mould my beaten head and knees.
New cars come swooping in like birds
To churn and chop the dust. A wireless,
Stuck in the sand, crackles lovesick words
As girls are roughed and raced
With whirling beach-balls in the sun.
What here avails my separate cloth,
My sober self, whose meaning contradicts
The sensual drama they enact in play?
'Hot Lips, Hot Lips', the throaty singer sighs:
A young man preens aloft and dives.

Is this the proper ending for a man?
The Pacific waves crash in upon the beach,
Roll and rise and inward stretch upon the beach.
It is December now and warm,
And yet my blood is cold, my shoulders slack;
In slow submission, I turn my body
Up to the sun, as on a rack,
Enduring comfort. In a dream,
I hear the cuckoo dance his double notes,
Among the harvest stooks like golden chessmen;
Each call, an age, a continent between.

No martyrdom, no wonder, no patent loss:
Is it for this mild ending that I
Have carried, all this way, my cross?

The Water Carrier

Twice daily I carried water from the spring,
Morning before leaving for school, and evening;
Balanced as a fulcrum between two buckets.

A bramble rough path ran to the river
Where one stepped carefully across slime-topped stones,
With corners abraded as bleakly white as bones.

At the widening pool (for washing and cattle)
Minute fish flickered as one dipped,
Circling to fill, with rust-tinged water.

The second or enamel bucket was for spring water
Which, after racing through a rushy meadow,
Came bubbling in a broken drain-pipe,

Corroded wafer thin with rust.
It ran so pure and cold, it fell
Like manacles of ice on the wrists.

One stood until the bucket brimmed
Inhaling the musty smell of unpicked berries,
That heavy greenness fostered by water.

[177]

Recovering the scene, I had hoped to stylize it,
Like the portrait of an Egyptian water-carrier:
Yet halt, entranced by slight but memoried life.

I sometimes come to take the water there,
Not as return or refuge, but some pure thing,
Some living source, half-imagined and half-real

Pulses in the fictive water that I feel.

The Trout

Flat on the bank I parted
Rushes to ease my hands
In the water without a ripple
And tilt them slowly downstream
To where he lay, tendril light,
In his fluid sensual dream.

Bodiless lord of creation
I hung briefly above him
Savouring my own absence
Senses expanding in the slow
Motion, the photographic calm
That grows before action.

As the curve of my hands
Swung under his body
He surged, with visible pleasure.
I was so preternaturally close
I could count every stipple
But still cast no shadow, until

The two palms crossed in a cage
Under the lightly pulsing gills.
Then (entering my own enlarged
Shape, which rode on the water)
I gripped. To this day I can
Taste his terror on my hands.

A Drink of Milk

In the girdered dark
of the byre, cattle move;
warm engines hushed
to a siding groove

before the switch flicks
down for milking.
In concrete partitions
they rattle their chains

while the farmhand eases
rubber tentacles to tug
lightly but rhythmically
on their swollen dugs

and up the pale cylinders
of the milking machine
mounts an untouched
steadily pulsing stream.

Only the tabby steals
to dip its radar whiskers
with old fashioned relish
in a chipped saucer

and before Seán lurches
to kick his boots off
in the night-silent kitchen
he draws a mug of froth

to settle on the sideboard
under the hoard of delft.
A pounding transistor shakes
the Virgin on her shelf

as he dreams towards bed.
A last glance at a magazine,
he puts the mug to his head,
grunts, and drains it clean.

Tim

Not those slim-flanked fillies
slender-ankled as models
glimpsed across the rails
through sunlong afternoons
as with fluent fetlocks
they devoured the miles

Nor at some Spring Show
a concourse of Clydesdales
waiting, huge as mammoths,
as enormous hirsute dolls,
for an incongruous rose to
blossom behind their ears

Nor that legendary Pegasus
leaping towards heaven:
only those hold my affection
who, stolid as weights,
stood in the rushy
meadows of my childhood

Or rumbled down lanes,
lumbering before carts.
Tim, the first horse I rode,
seasick on his barrel
back; the first to lip
bread from my hand.

I saw the end of your road.
You stood, with gouged eyeball
while our farmhand swabbed
the hurt socket out with
water and Jeyes Fluid:
as warm an object of

loving memory as any
who have followed me
to this day, denying
rhetoric with your patience,
forcing me to drink
from the trough of reality.

Like Dolmens round my Childhood, the Old People

Like dolmens round my childhood, the old people.

Jamie MacCrystal sang to himself,
A broken song without tune, without words;
He tipped me a penny every pension day,
Fed kindly crusts to winter birds.
When he died, his cottage was robbed,
Mattress and money box torn and searched.
Only the corpse they didn't disturb.

Maggie Owens was surrounded by animals,
A mongrel bitch and shivering pups,
Even in her bedroom a she-goat cried.
She was a well of gossip defiled,
Fanged chronicler of a whole countryside:
Reputed a witch, all I could find
Was her lonely need to deride.

The Nialls lived along a mountain lane
Where heather bells bloomed, clumps of foxglove.
All were blind, with Blind Pension and Wireless,
Dead eyes serpent-flicked as one entered
To shelter from a downpour of mountain rain.
Crickets chirped under the rocking hearthstone
Until the muddy sun shone out again.

Mary Moore lived in a crumbling gatehouse,
Famous as Pisa for its leaning gable.
Bag-apron and boots, she tramped the fields
Driving lean cattle from a miry stable.
A by-word for fierceness, she fell asleep
Over love stories, Red Star and Red Circle,
Dreamed of gypsy love rites, by firelight sealed.

Wild Billy Eagleson married a Catholic servant girl
When all his Loyal family passed on:
We danced round him shouting 'To Hell with King Billy,'
And dodged from the arc of his flailing blackthorn.
Forsaken by both creeds, he showed little concern
Until the Orange drums banged past in the summer
And bowler and sash aggressively shone.

Curate and doctor trudged to attend them,
Through knee-deep snow, through summer heat,
From main road to lane to broken path,
Gulping the mountain air with painful breath.
Sometimes they were found by neighbours,
Silent keepers of a smokeless hearth,
Suddenly cast in the mould of death.

Ancient Ireland, indeed! I was reared by her bedside,
The rune and the chant, evil eye and averted head,
Fomorian fierceness of family and local feud.
Gaunt figures of fear and of friendliness,
For years they trespassed on my dreams,
Until once, in a standing circle of stones,
I felt their shadows pass

Into that dark permanence of ancient forms.

A Welcoming Party

Wie war das möglich?

That final newsreel of the war:
A welcoming party of almost shades
Met us at the cinema door
Clicking what remained of their heels.

[184]

From nests of bodies like hatching eggs
Flickered insectlike hands and legs
And rose an ululation, terrible, shy;
Children conjugating the verb 'to die'.

One clamoured mutely of love
From a mouth like a burnt glove;
Others upheld hands bleak as begging bowls
Claiming the small change of our souls.

Some smiled at us as protectors.
Can these bones live?
Our parochial brand of innocence
Was all we had to give.

To be always at the periphery of incident
Gave my childhood its Irish dimension;
Yet doves of mercy, as doves of air,
Can falter here as anywhere.

That long dead Sunday in Armagh
I learned one meaning of total war
And went home to my Christian school
To kick a football through the air.

All Legendary Obstacles

All legendary obstacles lay between
Us, the long imaginary plain,
The monstrous ruck of mountains
And, swinging across the night,
Flooding the Sacramento, San Joaquin,
The hissing drift of winter rain.

All day I waited, shifting
Nervously from station to bar
As I saw another train sail
By, the San Francisco Chief or
Golden Gate, water dripping
From great flanged wheels.

At midnight you came, pale
Above the negro porter's lamp.
I was too blind with rain
And doubt to speak, but
Reached from the platform
Until our chilled hands met.

You had been travelling for days
With an old lady, who marked
A neat circle on the glass
With her glove, to watch us
Move into the wet darkness
Kissing, still unable to speak.

11 rue Daguerre

At night, sometimes, when I cannot sleep
I go to the *atelier* door
And smell the earth of the garden.

It exhales softly,
Especially now, approaching springtime,
When tendrils of green are plaited

Across the humus, desperately frail
In their passage against
The dark, unredeemed parcels of earth.

There is white light on the cobblestones
And in the apartment house opposite –
All four floors – silence.

In that stillness – soft but luminously exact,
A chosen light – I notice that
The tips of the lately grafted cherry-tree

Are a firm and lacquered black.

A Bright Day

for John McGahern

At times I see it, present
 As a bright day, or a hill,
The only way of saying something
 Luminously as possible.

Not the accumulated richness
 Of an old historical language –
That musk-deep odour!
 But a slow exactness

Which recreates experience
 By ritualizing its details –
Pale web of curtain, width
 Of deal table, till all

Takes on a witch-bright glow
 And even the clock on the mantel
Moves its hands in a fierce delight
 Of so, and so, and so.

The Road's End

May, and the air is light
On eye, on hand. As I take
The mountain road, my former step
Doubles mine, driving cattle
To the upland fields. Between
Shelving ditches of whitethorn
They sway their burdensome
Bodies, tempted at each turn
By hollows of sweet grass,
Pale clover, while memory,
A restive sally-switch, flicks
Across their backs.
                              The well
Is still there, a half-way mark
Between two cottages, opposite
The gate into Danaghy's field,
But above the protective dry-
Stone rim, the plaiting thorns
Have not been bill-hooked back
And a thick *glaur* floats.
No need to rush to head off
The cattle from sinking soft
Muzzles into leaf smelling
Spring water.

From the farm
Nearby, I hear a yard tap gush
And a collie bark, to check
My presence. Our farmhands
Lived there, wife and children
In twin white-washed cells,
A zinc roof burning in summer.
Now there is a kitchen extension
With radio aerial, rough outhouses
For coal and tractor. A housewife
Smiles good-day as I step through
The fluff and dust of her walled
Farmyard, solicited by raw-necked
Stalking turkeys
               to where cart
Ruts shape the ridge of a valley,
One of many among the switch-
Back hills of what old chroniclers
Called the Star Bog. Uncurling
Fern, white scut of bogcotton,
Spars of bleached bog fir jutting
From heather, make a landscape
So light in wash it must be learnt
Day by day, in shifting detail.
'I like to look across', said
Barney Horisk, leaning on his *slean*,
'And think of all the people
'Who have bin.'

Shards

Of a lost culture, the slopes
Are strewn with cabins, emptied
In my lifetime. Here the older
People sheltered, the Blind Nialls,
Big Ellen, who had been a Fair-
Day prostitute. The bushes cramp
To the evening wind as I reach
The road's end. Jamie MacCrystal
Lived in the final cottage,
A trim grove of mountain ash
Soughing protection round his walls
And bright painted gate. The thatch
Has slumped in, white dust of nettles
On the flags. Only the shed remains
In use for calves, although fuchsia
Bleeds by the wall, and someone
Has propped a yellow cartwheel
Against the door.

Return

From the bedroom you can see
straight to the fringe of the woods
with a cross staved gate to re-
enter childhood's world:
                              the pines
wait, dripping.

            Crumbling black-
berries, seized from a rack
of rusty leaves, maroon tents
of mushroom, pillars uprooting
with a dusty snap;

                  as the bucket
fills, a bird strikes from the bushes
and the cleats of your rubber boot crush
a yellow snail's shell to a smear
on the grass
            (while the wind starts
the carrion smell of the dead fox
staked as warning).

                  Seeing your former
self saunter up the garden path
afterwards, would you flinch,
acknowledging
                  that sensuality,
that innocence?

Clear the Way

Jimmy Drummond used bad language at school
All the four-letter words, like a drip from a drain.
At six he knew how little children were born
As well he might, since his mother bore nine,
Six after her soldier husband left for the wars

Under the motto of the Royal Irish, *Clear the Way!*
When his body returned from England
The authorities told them not to unscrew the lid
To see the remnants of Fusilier Drummond inside –
A chancey hand-grenade had left nothing to hide

And Jimmy's mother was pregnant at the graveside –
Clear the way, and nothing to hide.
Love came to her punctually each springtime,
Settled in the ditch under some labouring man:
'It comes over you, you have to lie down.'

Her only revenge on her hasty lovers
Was to call each child after its father,
Which the locals admired, and seeing her saunter
To collect the pension of her soldier husband
Trailed by her army of baby Irregulars.

Some of whom made soldiers for future wars
Some supplied factories in England.
Jimmy Drummond was the eldest but died younger than
                                                    any
When he fell from a scaffolding in Coventry
Condemned, like all his family, to *Clear the Way!*

[193]

The Country Fiddler

My uncle played the fiddle – more elegantly the violin –
A favourite at barn and cross-roads dance,
He knew *The Sailor's Bonnet* and *The Fowling Piece*.

Bachelor head of a house full of sisters,
Runner of poor racehorses, spendthrift,
He left for the New World in an old disgrace.

He left his fiddle in the rafters
When he sailed, never played afterwards;
A rural art silenced in the discord of Brooklyn.

A heavily-built man, tranquil-eyed as an ox,
He ran a wild speakeasy, and died of it.
During the depression many dossed in his cellar.

I attended his funeral in the Church of the Redemption,
Then, unexpected successor, reversed time
To return where he had been born.

During my schooldays the fiddle rusted
(The bridge fell away, the catgut snapped)
Reduced to a plaything stinking of stale rosin.

The country people asked if I also had music
(All the family had had) but the fiddle was in pieces
And the rafters remade, before I discovered my craft.

Twenty years afterwards, I saw the church again,
And promised to remember my burly godfather
And his rural craft, after this fashion:

So succession passes, through strangest hands.

The Cage

My father, the least happy
man I have known. His face
retained the pallor
of those who work underground:
the lost years in Brooklyn
listening to a subway
shudder the earth.

But a traditional Irishman
who (released from his grille
in the Clark St I.R.T.)
drank neat whiskey until
he reached the only element
he felt at home in
any longer: brute oblivion.

And yet picked himself
up, most mornings,
to march down the street
extending his smile

[195]

to all sides of the good
(non-negro) neigbourhood
belled by St Teresa's church.

When he came back
we walked together
across fields of Garvaghey
to see hawthorn on the summer
hedges, as though
he had never left;
a bend of the road

which still sheltered
primroses. But we
did not smile in
the shared complicity
of a dream, for when
weary Odysseus returns
Telemachus must leave.

Often as I descend
into subway or underground
I see his bald head behind
the bars of the small booth;
the mark of an old car
accident beating on his
ghostly forehead.

Coming Events

In the Stadsmuzeum at Bruges, there is a picture by Gerard
David of a man being flayed. Four craftsmen are concerned
with the figure on the table: one is opening the left arm,
another lifting away the right nipple, a third incising the
right arm while the last (his knife caught between his
teeth) is unwinding the results of his labour so as to
display the rich network of veins under the skin of the left
leg. The only expression in the faces of those looking on is
a mild admiration: the Burgmeister has caught up the
white folds of his ermine gown and is gazing into the
middle distance. It is difficult even to say that there is any
expression on the face of the victim, although his teeth are
gritted and the cords attaching his wrists to the legs of the
table are stretched tight. The whole scene may be intended
as an allegory of human suffering but what the line of
perspective leads us to admire is the brown calfskin of the
principal executioner's boots.

Last Journey

I.M. James Montague

We stand together
on the windy platform;
how crisp the rails
running out of sight
through the wet fields!

Carney, the station master,
is peering over
his frosted window:
the hand of the signal
points down.

Crowned with churns
a cart creaks up the
incline of Main Street
to the sliding doors
of the Co-op.

A smell of coal,
the train is coming . . .
you climb slowly in,
propped by my hand to
a seat, back to the engine,

and we leave, waving
a plume of black smoke
over the rushy meadows,
small hills & hidden villages –
Beragh, Carrickmore,

Pomeroy, Fintona –
placenames that sigh
like a pressed melodeon
across this forgotten
Northern landscape.

Penal Rock: Altamuskin

To learn the massrock's lesson, leave your car,
Descend frost gripped steps to where
A humid moss overlaps the valley floor.
Crisp as a pistol-shot, the winter air
Recalls poor Tagues, folding the nap of their frieze
Under one knee, long suffering as beasts,
But parched for that surviving sign of grace,
The bog-Latin murmur of their priest.
A crude stone oratory, carved by a cousin,
Commemorates the place. For two hundred years
People of our name have sheltered in this glen
But now all have left. A few flowers
Wither on the altar, so I melt a ball of snow
From the hedge into their rusty tin before I go.

Mad Sweeny

A wet silence.
Wait under trees,
muscles tense,
ear lifted, eye alert.

Lungs clear.
A nest of senses
stirring awake –
human beast!

[199]

A bird lights:
two claw prints.
Two leaves shift:
a small wind.

Beneath, white
rush of current,
stone chattering
between high banks.

Occasional shrill
of a bird, squirrel
trampolining along
a springy branch.

Start a slow
dance, lifting
a foot, planting
a heel to celebrate

greenness, rain
spatter on skin,
the humid pull
of the earth.

The whole world
turning in wet
and silence, a
damp mill wheel.

Windharp

for Patrick Collins

The sounds of Ireland,
that restless whispering
you never get away
from, seeping out of
low bushes and grass,
heatherbells and fern,
wrinkling bog pools,
scraping tree branches,
light hunting cloud,
sound hounding sight,
a hand ceaselessly
combing and stroking
the landscape, till
the valley gleams
like the pile upon
a mountain pony's coat.

Tracks

I

The vast bedroom
a hall of air,
our linked bodies
lying there.

II

As I turn to kiss
your long, black
hair, small breasts,
heat flares from
your fragrant skin,
your eyes widen as
deeper, more certain
and often, I enter
to search possession
of where your being
hides in flesh.

III

Behind our eyelids
a landscape opens,
a violet horizon
pilgrims labour across,
a sky of colours
that change, explode
a fantail of stars
the mental lightning
of sex illuminating
the walls of the skull;
a floating pleasure dome.

IV

I shall miss you
creaks the mirror
into which the scene
shortly disappears:
the vast bedroom
a hall of air, the
tracks of our bodies
fading there, while
giggling maids push
a trolley of fresh
linen down the corridor.

Herbert Street Revisited

for Madeleine

I

A light is burning late
in this Georgian Dublin street:
someone is leading our old lives!

And our black cat scampers again
through the wet grass of the convent garden
upon his masculine errands.

The pubs shut: a released bull,
Behan shoulders up the street,
topples into our basement, roaring 'John!'

A pony and donkey cropped flank
by flank under the trees opposite;
short neck up, long neck down,

as Nurse Mullen knelt by her bedside
to pray for her lost Mayo hills,
the bruised bodies of Easter Volunteers.

Animals, neighbours, treading the pattern
of one time and place into history,
like our early marriage, while

tall windows looked down upon us
from walls flushed light pink or salmon
watching and enduring succession.

II

As I leave, you whisper,
'don't betray our truth'
and like a ghost dancer,
invoking a lost tribal strength
I halt in tree-fed darkness
to summon back our past,
and celebrate a love that eased
so kindly the dying bone,
enabling the spirit to sing
of old happiness, when alone.

III

So put the leaves back on the tree,
put the tree back in the ground,
let Brendan trundle his corpse down
the street singing, like Molly Malone.

Let the black cat, tiny emissary
of our happiness, streak again
through the darkness, to fall soft
clawed into a landlord's dustbin.

Let Nurse Mullen take the last
train to Westport, and die upright
in her chair, facing a window
warm with the blue slopes of Nephin.

And let the pony and donkey come –
look, someone has left the gate open –
like hobbyhorses linked in
the slow motion of a dream

parading side by side, down
the length of Herbert Street,
rising and falling, lifting
their hooves through the moonlight.

Sunset

from the *Félire Oengus*

In Loch Lene
a queen went swimming;
a redgold salmon
flowed into her
at full of evening.

The Silver Flask

Sweet, though short, our
hours as a family together.
Driving across dark mountains
to Midnight Mass in Fivemiletown,
lights coming up in the valleys
as in the days of Carleton.

Tussocks of heather brown
in the headlights; our mother
stowed in the back, a tartan
rug wrapped round her knees,
patiently listening as father sang,
and the silver flask went round.

Chorus after chorus of the *Adoremus*
to shorten the road before us,
till *we see amidst the winter's snows*
the festive lights of the small town
and from the choirloft an organ booms
angels we have heard on high, with

my father joining warmly in,
his broken tenor soaring, faltering,
a legend in dim bars of Brooklyn
(that sacramental moment of stillness
among exiled, disgruntled men)
now raised vehemently once again

in the valleys he had sprung from,
startling the stiff congregation
with fierce blasts of song, while
our mother sat silent beside him,
sad but proud, an unaccustomed
blush mantling her wan countenance.

Then driving slowly home,
tongues crossed with the communion
wafer, snowflakes melting in
the car's hungry headlights,
till we reach the warm kitchen
and the spirits round again.

The family circle briefly restored
nearly twenty lonely years after
that last Christmas in Brooklyn,
under the same tinsel of decorations
so carefully hoarded by our mother
in the cabin trunk of a Cunard liner.

MICHAEL LONGLEY   1939–

Leaving Inishmore

Rain and sunlight and the boat between them
Shifted whole hillsides through the afternoon –
Quiet variations on an urgent theme
Reminding me now that we left too soon
The island awash in wave and anthem.

Miles from the brimming enclave of the bay
I hear again the Atlantic's voices,
The gulls above us as we pulled away –
So munificent their final noises
These are the broadcasts from our holiday.

Oh, the crooked walkers on that tilting floor!
And the girls singing on the upper deck
Whose hair took the light like a downpour –
Interim nor change of scene shall shipwreck
Those folk on the move between shore and shore.

Summer and solstice as the seasons turn
Anchor our boat in a perfect standstill,
The harbour wall of Inishmore astern
Where the Atlantic waters overspill –
I shall name this the point of no return

Lest that excursion out of light and heat
Take on a January idiom –
Our ocean icebound when the year is hurt,
Wintertime past cure – the curriculum
Vitae of sailors and the sick at heart.

No Continuing City

My hands here, gentle, where her breasts begin,
My picture in her eyes –
It is time for me to recognize
This new dimension, my last girl.
So, to set my house in order, I imagine
Photographs, advertisements – the old lies,
The lumber of my soul –

All that is due for spring cleaning,
Everything that soul-destroys.
Into the open I bring
Girls who linger still in photostat
(For whom I was so many different boys) –
I explode their myths before it is too late,
Their promises I detonate –

There is quite a lot that I can do . . .
I leave them – are they six or seven, two or three? –
Locked in their small geographies.
The hillocks of their bodies' lovely shires
(Whose all weathers I have walked through)
Acre by acre recede entire
To summer country.

From collision to eclipse their case is closed.
Who took me by surprise

Like comets first – now, failing to ignite,
They constellate such uneventful skies,
Their stars arranged each night
In the old stories
Which I successfully have diagnosed.

Though they momentarily survive
In my delays,
They neither cancel nor improve
My continuing city with old ways,
Familiar avenues to love –
Down my one way streets (it is time to finish)
Their eager syllables diminish.

Though they call out from the suburbs
Of experience – they know how that disturbs! –
Or, already tending towards home,
Prepare to hitch-hike on the kerbs,
Their bags full of dear untruths –
I am their medium
And I take the words out of their mouths.

From today new hoardings crowd my eyes,
Pasted over my ancient histories
Which (I must be cruel to be kind)
Only gale or cloudburst now discover,
Ripping the billboard of my mind –
Oh, there my lovers,
There my dead no longer advertise.

I transmit from the heart a closing broadcast
To my girl, my bride, my wife-to-be –
I tell her she is welcome,
Advising her to make this last,
To be sure of finding room in me
(I embody bed and breakfast) –
To eat and drink me out of house and home.

Persephone

I

I see as through a skylight in my brain
The mole strew its buildings in the rain,

The swallows turn above their broken homes
And all my acres in delirium.

II

Straitjacketed by cold and numbskulled
Now sleep the welladjusted and the skilled –

The bat folds its wing like a winter leaf,
The squirrel in its hollow holds aloof.

III

The weasel and ferret, the stoat and fox
Move hand in glove across the equinox.

I can tell how softly their footsteps go –
Their footsteps borrow silence from the snow.

In Memoriam

My father, let no similes eclipse
Where crosses like some forest simplified
Sink roots into my mind; the slow sands
Of your history delay till through your eyes
I read you like a book. Before you died,
Re-enlisting with all the broken soldiers
You bent beneath your rucksack, near collapse,
In anecdote rehearsed and summarized
These words I write in memory. Let yours
And other heartbreaks play into my hands.

Now I see in close-up, in my mind's eye,
The cracked and splintered dead for pity's sake
Each dismal evening predecease the sun,
You, looking death and nightmare in the face
With your kilt, harmonica and gun,
Grow older in a flash, but none the wiser
(Who, following the wrong queue at The Palace,
Have joined the London Scottish by mistake),
Your nineteen years uncertain if and why
Belgium put the kibosh on the Kaiser.

[215]

Between the corpses and the soup canteens
You swooned away, watching your future spill.
But, as it was, your proper funeral urn
Had mercifully smashed to smithereens,
To shrapnel shards that sliced your testicle.
That instant I, your most unlikely son,
In No Man's Land was surely left for dead,
Blotted out from your far horizon.
As your voice now is locked inside my head,
I yet was held secure, waiting my turn.

Finally, that lousy war was over.
Stranded in France and in need of proof
You hunted down experimental lovers,
Persuading chorus girls and countesses:
This, father, the last confidence you spoke.
In my twentieth year your old wounds woke
As cancer. Lodging under the same roof
Death was a visitor who hung about,
Strewing the house with pills and bandages,
Till he chose to put your spirit out.

Though they overslept the sequence of events
Which ended with the ambulance outside,
You lingering in the hall, your bowels on fire,
Tears in your eyes, and all your medals spent,
I summon girls who packed at last and went
Underground with you. Their souls again on hire,
Now those lost wives as recreated brides
Take shape before me, materialize.
On the verge of light and happy legend
They lift their skirts like blinds across your eyes.

Wounds

Here are two pictures from my father's head –
I have kept them like secrets until now:
First, the Ulster Division at the Somme
Going over the top with 'Fuck the Pope!'
'No Surrender!': a boy about to die,
Screaming 'Give 'em one for the Shankill!'
'Wilder than Gurkhas' were my father's words
Of admiration and bewilderment.
Next comes the London-Scottish padre
Resettling kilts with his swagger-stick,
With a stylish backhand and a prayer.
Over a landscape of dead buttocks
My father followed him for fifty years.
At last, a belated casualty,
He said – lead traces flaring till they hurt –
'I am dying for King and Country, slowly.'
I touched his hand, his thin head I touched.

Now, with military honours of a kind,
With his badges, his medals like rainbows,
His spinning compass, I bury beside him
Three teenage soldiers, bellies full of
Bullets and Irish beer, their flies undone.
A packet of Woodbines I throw in,
A lucifer, the Sacred Heart of Jesus
Paralysed as heavy guns put out
The night-light in a nursery for ever;

Also a bus-conductor's uniform –
He collapsed beside his carpet-slippers
Without a murmur, shot through the head
By a shivering boy who wandered in
Before they could turn the television down
Or tidy away the supper dishes.
To the children, to a bewildered wife,
I think 'Sorry Missus' was what he said.

Letter to Derek Mahon

And did we come into our own
When, minus muse and lexicon,
We traced in August sixty-nine
Our imaginary Peace Line
Around the burnt-out houses of
The Catholics we'd scarcely loved,
Two Sisyphuses come to budge
The sticks and stones of an old grudge,

Two poetic conservatives
In the city of guns and long knives,
Our ears receiving then and there
The stereophonic nightmare
Of the Shankill and the Falls,
Our matches struck on crumbling walls
To light us as we moved at last
Through the back alleys of Belfast?

Why it mattered to have you here
You who journeyed to Inishere
With me, years back, one Easter when
With MacIntyre and the lone Dane
Our footsteps lifted up the larks,
Echoing off those western rocks
And down that darkening arcade
Hung with the failures of our trade,

Will understand. We were tongue-tied
Companions of the island's dead
In the graveyard among the dunes,
Eavesdroppers on conversations
With a Jesus who spoke Irish –
We were strangers in that parish,
Black tea with bacon and cabbage
For our sacraments and pottage,

Dank blankets making up our Lent
Till, islanders ourselves, we bent
Our knees and cut the watery sod
From the lazy-bed where slept a God
We couldn't count among our friends,
Although we'd taken in our hands
Splinters of driftwood nailed and stuck
On the rim of the Atlantic.

That was Good Friday years ago –
How persistent the undertow
Slapped by currachs ferrying stones,
Moonlight glossing the confusions
Of its each bilingual wave – yes,
We would have lingered there for less . . .
Six islanders for a ten bob note
Rowed us out to the anchored boat.

Letter to Seamus Heaney

From Carrigskeewaun in Killadoon
I write, although I'll see you soon,
Hoping this fortnight detonates
Your year in the United States,
Offering you by way of welcome
To the sick counties we call home
The mystical point at which I tire
Of Calor gas and a turf fire.

Till we talk again in Belfast
Pleasanter far to leave the past
Across three acres and two brooks
On holiday in a post box
Which dripping fuchsia bells surround,
Its back to the prevailing wind,
And where sanderlings from Iceland
Court the breakers, take my stand,

Disinfecting with a purer air
That small subconscious cottage where
The Irish poet slams his door
On slow-worm, toad and adder:
Beneath these racing skies it is
A tempting stance indeed – *ipsis*
Hibernicis hiberniores –
Except that we know the old stories,

The midden of cracked hurley sticks
Tied to recall the crucifix,
Of broken bones and lost scruples,
The blackened hearth, the blazing gable's
Telltale cinder where we may
Scorch our shins until that day
We sleepwalk through a No Man's Land
Lipreading to an Orange band.

Continually, therefore, we rehearse
Goodbyes to all our characters
And, since both would have it both ways,
On the oily roll of calmer seas
Launch coffin-ship and life-boat,
Body with soul thus kept afloat,
Mind open like a half-door
To the speckled hill, the plovers' shore.

So let it be the lapwing's cry
That lodges in the throat as I
Raise its alarum from the mud.
Seeking for your sake to conclude
Ulster Poet our Union Title

And prolong this sad recital
By leaving careful footprints round
A wind-encircled burial mound.

Skara Brae

for Denis and Sheila Smyth

A window into the ground,
The bumpy lawn in section,
An exploded view
Through middens, through lives,

The thatch of grass roots,
The gravelly roof compounding
Periwinkles, small bones,
A calendar of meals,

The thread between sepulchre
And home a broken necklace,
Knuckles, dice scattering
At the warren's core,

Pebbles the tide washes
That conceded for so long
Living room, the hard beds,
The table made of stone.

Swans Mating

Even now I wish that you had been there
Sitting beside me on the riverbank:
The cob and his pen sailing in rhythm
Until their small heads met and the final
Heraldic moment dissolved in ripples.

This was a marriage and a baptism,
A holding of breath, nearly a drowning,
Wings spread wide for balance where he trod,
Her feathers full of water and her neck
Under the water like a bar of light.

Caravan

A rickety chimney suggests
The diminutive stove,
Children perhaps, the pots
And pans adding up to love –

So much concentrated under
The low roof, the windows
Shuttered against snow and wind,
That you would be magnified

(If you were there) by the dark,
Wearing it like an apron
And revolving in your hands
As weather in a glass dome,

The blizzard, the day beyond
And – tiny, barely in focus –
Me disappearing out of view
On probably the only horse,

Cantering off to the right
To collect the week's groceries,
Or to be gone for good
Having drawn across my eyes

Like a curtain all that light
And the snow, my history
Stiffening with the tea towels
Hung outside the door to dry.

The Lodger

The lodger is writing a novel.
We give him the run of the house
But he occupies my mind as well –
An attic, a lumber-room
For his typewriter, notebooks,
The slowly accumulating pages.

At the end of each four-fingered
Suffering line the angelus rings –
A hundred noons and sunsets
As we lie here whispering,
Careful not to curtail our lives
Or change the names he has given us.

Fleance

I entered with a torch before me
And cast my shadow on the backcloth
Momentarily: a handful of words,
One bullet with my initials on it –
And that got stuck in a property tree.

I would have caught it between my teeth
Or, a true professional, stood still
While the two poetic murderers
Pinned my silhouette to history
In a shower of accurate daggers.

But as any illusionist might
Unfasten the big sack of darkness,
The ropes and handcuffs, and emerge
Smoking a nonchalant cigarette,
I escaped – only to lose myself.

It took me a lifetime to explore
The dusty warren beneath the stage
With its trapdoor opening on to
All that had happened above my head
Like noises-off or distant weather.

In the empty auditorium I bowed
To one preoccupied caretaker
And, without removing my make-up,
Hurried back to the digs where Banquo
Sat up late with a hole in his head.

Man Lying on a Wall

Homage to L. S. Lowry

You could draw a straight line from the heels,
Through calves, buttocks and shoulderblades
To the back of the head: pressure points
That bear the enormous weight of the sky.
Should you take away the supporting structure
The result would be a miracle or
An extremely clever conjuring trick.
As it is, the man lying on the wall
Is wearing the serious expression
Of popes and kings in their final slumber,
His deportment not dissimilar to
Their stiff, reluctant exits from this world
Above the shoulders of the multitude.

It is difficult to judge whether or not
He is sleeping or merely disinclined
To arrive punctually at the office
Or to return home in time for his tea.
He is wearing a pinstripe suit, black shoes
And a bowler hat: on the pavement
Below him, like a relic or something
He is trying to forget, his briefcase
With everybody's initials on it.

The Linen Workers

Christ's teeth ascended with him into heaven:
Through a cavity in one of his molars
The wind whistles: he is fastened for ever
By his exposed canines to a wintry sky.

I am blinded by the blaze of that smile
And by the memory of my father's false teeth
Brimming in their tumbler: they wore bubbles
And, outside of his body, a deadly grin.

When they massacred the ten linen workers
There fell on the road beside them spectacles,
Wallets, small change, and a set of dentures:
Blood, food particles, the bread, the wine.

[227]

Before I can bury my father once again
I must polish the spectacles, balance them
Upon his nose, fill his pockets with money
And into his dead mouth slip the set of teeth.

Second Sight

My father's mother had the second sight.
Flanders began at the kitchen window –
The mangle rusting in No Man's Land, gas
Turning the antimacassars yellow
When it blew the wrong way from the salient.

In bandages, on crutches, reaching home
Before his letters, my father used to find
The front door on the latch, his bed airing.
'I watched my son going over the top.
He was carrying flowers out of the smoke.'

I have brought the *Pocket Guide to London*,
My *Map of the Underground*, an address –
A lover looking for somewhere to live,
A ghost among ghosts of aunts and uncles
Who crowd around me to give directions.

Where is my father's house, where my father?
If I could walk in on my grandmother
She'd see right through me and the hallway
And the miles of cloud and sky to Ireland.
'You have crossed the water to visit me.'

[228]

The Third Light

The sexton is opening up the grave,
Lining with mossy cushions and couch grass
This shaft of light, entrance to the earth
Where I kneel to marry you again,
My elbows in darkness as I explore
From my draughty attic your last bedroom.
Then I vanish into the roof space.

I have handed over to him your pain
And your preference for Cyprus sherry,
Your spry quotations from the *Daily Mail*
With its crossword solved in ink, your limp
And pills, your scatter of cigarette butts
And last-minute humorous spring-cleaning
Of a corner of a shelf in his cupboard.

You spent his medals like a currency,
Always refusing the third light, afraid
Of the snipers who would extinguish it.
Waiting to scramble hand in hand with him
Out of the shell hole, did you imagine
A Woodbine passing to and fro, a face
That stabilizes like a smoke ring?

SEAMUS HEANEY   1939–

Follower

My father worked with a horse-plough,
His shoulders globed like a full sail strung
Between the shafts and the furrow.
The horses strained at his clicking tongue.

An expert. He would set the wing
And fit the bright steel-pointed sock.
The sod rolled over without breaking.
At the headrig, with a single pluck

Of reins, the sweating team turned round
And back into the land. His eye
Narrowed and angled at the ground,
Mapping the furrow exactly.

I stumbled in his hob-nailed wake,
Fell sometimes on the polished sod;
Sometimes he rode me on his back
Dipping and rising to his plod.

I wanted to grow up and plough,
To close one eye, stiffen my arm.
All I ever did was follow
In his broad shadow round the farm.

I was a nuisance, tripping, falling,
Yapping always. But today
It is my father who keeps stumbling
Behind me, and will not go away.

The Diviner

Cut from the green hedge a forked hazel stick
That he held tight by the arms of the V:
Circling the terrain, hunting the pluck
Of water, nervous, but professionally

Unfussed. The pluck came sharp as a sting.
The rod jerked down with precise convulsions,
Spring water suddenly broadcasting
Through a green aerial its secret stations.

The bystanders would ask to have a try.
He handed them the rod without a word.
It lay dead in their grasp till nonchalantly
He gripped expectant wrists. The hazel stirred.

Personal Helicon

for Michael Longley

As a child, they could not keep me from wells
And old pumps with buckets and windlasses.
I loved the dark drop, the trapped sky, the smells
Of waterweed, fungus and dank moss.

[234]

One, in a brickyard, with a rotted board top.
I savoured the rich crash when a bucket
Plummeted down at the end of a rope.
So deep you saw no reflection in it.

A shallow one under a dry stone ditch
Fructified like any aquarium.
When you dragged out long roots from the soft mulch
A white face hovered over the bottom.

Others had echoes, gave back your own call
With a clean new music in it. And one
Was scaresome for there, out of ferns and tall
Foxgloves, a rat slapped across my reflection.

Now, to pry into roots, to finger slime,
To stare, big-eyed Narcissus, into some spring
Is beneath all adult dignity. I rhyme
To see myself, to set the darkness echoing.

The Forge

All I know is a door into the dark.
Outside, old axles and iron hoops rusting;
Inside, the hammered anvil's short-pitched ring,
The unpredictable fantail of sparks
Or hiss when a new shoe toughens in water.
The anvil must be somewhere in the centre,
Horned as a unicorn, at one end square,

Set there immovable: an altar
Where he expends himself in shape and music.
Sometimes, leather-aproned, hairs in his nose,
He leans out on the jamb, recalls a clatter
Of hoofs where traffic is flashing in rows;
Then grunts and goes in, with a slam and flick
To beat real iron out, to work the bellows.

Thatcher

Bespoke for weeks, he turned up some morning
Unexpectedly, his bicycle slung
With a light ladder and a bag of knives.
He eyed the old rigging, poked at the eaves,

Opened and handled sheaves of lashed wheat-straw.
Next, the bundled rods: hazel and willow
Were flicked for weight, twisted in case they'd snap.
It seemed he spent the morning warming up:

Then fixed the ladder, laid out well honed blades
And snipped at straw and sharpened ends of rods
That, bent in two, made a white-pronged staple
For pinning down his world, handful by handful.

Couchant for days on sods above the rafters
He shaved and flushed the butts, stitched all together
Into a sloped honeycomb, a stubble patch,
And left them gaping at his Midas touch.

SEAMUS HEANEY

The Peninsula

When you have nothing more to say, just drive
For a day all round the peninsula.
The sky is tall as over a runway,
The land without marks so you will not arrive

But pass through, though always skirting landfall.
At dusk, horizons drink down sea and hill,
The ploughed field swallows the whitewashed gable
And you're in the dark again. Now recall

The glazed foreshore and silhouetted log,
That rock where breakers shredded into rags,
The leggy birds stilted on their own legs,
Islands riding themselves out into the fog

And drive back home, still with nothing to say
Except that now you will uncode all landscapes
By this: things founded clean on their own shapes,
Water and ground in their extremity.

Requiem for the Croppies

The pockets of our greatcoats full of barley –
No kitchens on the run, no striking camp –
We moved quick and sudden in our own country.
The priest lay behind ditches with the tramp.
A people, hardly marching – on the hike –
We found new tactics happening each day:
We'd cut through reins and rider with the pike
And stampede cattle into infantry,
Then retreat through hedges where cavalry must be
                                        thrown.
Until, on Vinegar Hill, the fatal conclave.
Terraced thousands died, shaking scythes at cannon.
The hillside blushed, soaked in our broken wave.
They buried us without shroud or coffin
And in August the barley grew up out of the grave.

Night Drive

The smells of ordinariness
Were new on the night drive through France:
Rain and hay and woods on the air
Made warm draughts in the open car.

Signposts whitened relentlessly.
Montreuil, Abbéville, Beauvais
Were promised, promised, came and went,
Each place granting its name's fulfilment.

[238]

A combine groaning its way late
Bled seeds across its work-light.
A forest fire smouldered out.
One by one small cafés shut.

I thought of you continuously
A thousand miles south where Italy
Laid its loin to France on the darkened sphere.
Your ordinariness was renewed there.

The Given Note

On the most westerly Blasket
In a dry-stone hut
He got this air out of the night.

Strange noises were heard
By others who followed, bits of a tune
Coming in on loud weather

Though nothing like melody.
He blamed their fingers and ear
As unpractised, their fiddling easy

For he had gone alone into the island
And brought back the whole thing.
The house throbbed like his full violin.

[239]

So whether he calls it spirit music
Or not, I don't care. He took it
Out of wind off mid-Atlantic.

Still he maintains, from nowhere.
It comes off the bow gravely,
Rephrases itself into the air.

The Plantation

Any point in that wood
Was a centre, birch trunks
Ghosting your bearings,
Improvising charmed rings

Wherever you stopped.
Though you walked a straight line
It might be a circle you travelled
With toadstools and stumps

Always repeating themselves.
Or did you re-pass them?
Here were blaeberries quilting the floor,
The black char of a fire

And having found them once
You were sure to find them again.
Someone had always been there
Though always you were alone.

[240]

Lovers, birdwatchers,
Campers, gipsies and tramps
Left some trace of their trades
Or their excrement.

Hedging the road so
It invited all comers
To the hush and the mush
Of its whispering treadmill,

Its limits defined,
So they thought, from outside.
They must have been thankful
For the hum of the traffic

If they ventured in
Past the picnickers' belt
Or began to recall
Tales of fog on the mountains.

You had to come back
To learn how to lose yourself,
To be pilot and stray – witch,
Hansel and Gretel in one.

Bogland

for T. P. Flanagan

We have no prairies
To slice a big sun at evening –
Everywhere the eye concedes to
Encroaching horizon,

Is wooed into the cyclops' eye
Of a tarn. Our unfenced country
Is bog that keeps crusting
Between the sights of the sun.

They've taken the skeleton
Of the Great Irish Elk
Out of the peat, set it up
An astounding crate full of air.

Butter sunk under
More than a hundred years
Was recovered salty and white.
The ground itself is kind, black butter

Melting and opening underfoot,
Missing its last definition
By millions of years.
They'll never dig coal here,

Only the waterlogged trunks
Of great firs, soft as pulp.
Our pioneers keep striking
Inwards and downwards,

Every layer they strip
Seems camped on before.
The bogholes might be Atlantic seepage.
The wet centre is bottomless.

The Other Side

I

Thigh-deep in sedge and marigolds
a neighbour laid his shadow
on the stream, vouching

'It's poor as Lazarus, that ground,'
and brushed away
among the shaken leafage:

I lay where his lea sloped
to meet our fallow,
nested on moss and rushes,

my ear swallowing
his fabulous, biblical dismissal,
that tongue of chosen people.

When he would stand like that
on the other side, white-haired,
swinging his blackthorn

at the marsh weeds,
he prophesied above our scraggy acres,
then turned away

towards his promised furrows
on the hill, a wake of pollen
drifting to our bank, next season's tares.

II

For days we would rehearse
each patriarchal dictum:
Lazarus, the Pharaoh, Solomon

and David and Goliath rolled
magnificently, like loads of hay
too big for our small lanes,

or faltered on a rut –
'Your side of the house, I believe,
hardly rule by the book at all.'

His brain was a whitewashed kitchen
hung with texts, swept tidy
as the body o' the kirk.

III

Then sometimes when the rosary was dragging
mournfully on in the kitchen
we would hear his step round the gable

though not until after the litany
would the knock come to the door
and the casual whistle strike up

on the doorstep. 'A right-looking night,'
he might say, 'I was dandering by
and says I, I might as well call.'

But now I stand behind him
in the dark yard, in the moan of prayers.
He puts a hand in a pocket

or taps a little tune with the blackthorn
shyly, as if he were party to
lovemaking or a stranger's weeping.

Should I slip away, I wonder,
or go up and touch his shoulder
and talk about the weather

or the price of grass-seed?

The Tollund Man

I

Some day I will go to Aarhus
To see his peat-brown head,
The mild pods of his eye-lids,
His pointed skin cap.

In the flat country nearby
Where they dug him out,
His last gruel of winter seeds
Caked in his stomach,

Naked except for
The cap, noose and girdle,
I will stand a long time.
Bridegroom to the goddess,

She tightened her torc on him
And opened her fen,
Those dark juices working
Him to a saint's kept body,

Trove of the turfcutters'
Honeycombed workings.
Now his stained face
Reposes at Aarhus.

II

I could risk blasphemy,
Consecrate the cauldron bog
Our holy ground and pray
Him to make germinate

The scattered, ambushed
Flesh of labourers,
Stockinged corpses
Laid out in the farmyards,

Tell-tale skin and teeth
Flecking the sleepers
Of four young brothers, trailed
For miles along the lines.

III

Something of his sad freedom
As he rode the tumbril
Should come to me, driving,
Saying the names

Tollund, Grauballe, Nebelgard,
Watching the pointing hands
Of country people,
Not knowing their tongue.

Out there in Jutland
In the old man-killing parishes
I will feel lost,
Unhappy and at home.

Summer Home

I

Was it wind off the dumps
or something in heat

dogging us, the summer gone sour,
a fouled nest incubating somewhere?

Whose fault, I wondered, inquisitor
of the possessed air.

To realize suddenly,
whip off the mat

that was larval, moving –
and scald, scald, scald.

II

Bushing the door, my arms full
of wild cherry and rhododendron,
I hear her small lost weeping
through the hall, that bells and hoarsens
on my name, my name.

O love, here is the blame.

The loosened flowers between us
gather in, compose
for a May altar of sorts.
These frank and falling blooms
soon taint to a sweet chrism.

Attend. Anoint the wound.

III

O we tented our wound all right
under the homely sheet

and lay as if the cold flat of a blade
had winded us.

More and more I postulate
thick healings, like now

as you bend in the shower
water lives down the tilting stoups of your breasts.

IV

With a final
unmusical drive
long grains begin
to open and split

ahead and once more
we sap
the white, trodden
path to the heart.

[249]

V

My children weep out the hot foreign night.
We walk the floor, my foul mouth takes it out
On you and we lie stiff till dawn
Attends the pillow, and the maize, and vine

That holds its filling burden to the light.
Yesterday rocks sang when we tapped
Stalactites in the cave's old, dripping dark –
Our love calls tiny as a tuning fork.

Mossbawn: Two Poems in Dedication

for Mary Heaney

1. Sunlight

There was a sunlit absence.
The helmeted pump in the yard
heated its iron,
water honeyed

in the slung bucket
and the sun stood
like a griddle cooling
against the wall

of each long afternoon.
So, her hands scuffled
over the bakeboard,
the reddening stove

sent its plaque of heat
against her where she stood
in a floury apron
by the window.

Now she dusts the board
with a goose's wing,
now sits, broad-lapped,
with whitened nails

and measling shins:
here is a space
again, the scone rising
to the tick of two clocks.

And here is love
like a tinsmith's scoop
sunk past its gleam
in the meal-bin.

2. The Seed Cutters

They seem hundreds of years away. Breughel,
You'll know them if I can get them true.
They kneel under the hedge in a half-circle
Behind a windbreak wind is breaking through.

[251]

They are the seed cutters. The tuck and frill
Of leaf-sprout is on the seed potatoes
Buried under that straw. With time to kill
They are taking their time. Each sharp knife goes
Lazily halving each root that falls apart
In the palm of the hand: a milky gleam,
And, at the centre, a dark watermark.
O calendar customs! Under the broom
Yellowing over them, compose the frieze
With all of us there, our anonymities.

A Drink of Water

She came every morning to draw water
Like an old bat staggering up the field:
The pump's whooping cough, the bucket's clatter
And slow diminuendo as it filled,
Announced her. I recall
Her grey apron, the pocked white enamel
Of the brimming bucket, and the treble
Creak of her voice like the pump's handle.
Nights when a full moon lifted past her gable
It fell back through her window and would lie
Into the water set out on the table.
Where I have dipped to drink again, to be
Faithful to the admonishment on her cup,
Remember the Giver fading off the lip.

A Postcard from North Antrim

In memory of Sean Armstrong

A lone figure is waving
From the thin line of a bridge
Of ropes and slats, slung
Dangerously out between
The cliff-top and the pillar rock.
A nineteenth-century wind.
Dulse-pickers. Sea campions.

A postcard for you, Sean,
And that's you, swinging alone,
Antic, half-afraid,
In your gallowglass's beard
And swallow-tail of serge:
The Carrick-a-Rede Rope Bridge
Ghost-written on sepia.

Or should it be your houseboat
Ethnically furnished,
Redolent of grass?
Should we discover you
Beside those warm-planked, democratic wharves
Among the twilights and guitars
Of Sausalito?

Drop-out on a come-back,
Prince of no-man's land
With your head in clouds or sand,
You were the clown
Social worker of the town
Until your candid forehead stopped
A pointblank teatime bullet.

Get up from your blood on the floor.
Here's another boat
In grass by the lough shore,
Turf smoke, a wired hen-run –
Your local, hoped for, unfound commune.
Now recite me *William Bloat*,
Sing of *the Calabar*

Or of Henry Joy McCracken
Who kissed his Mary Ann
On the gallows at Cornmarket.
Or Ballycastle Fair.
'Give us the raw bar!'
'Sing it by brute force
If you forget the air.'

Yet something in your voice
Stayed nearly shut.
Your voice was a harassed pulpit
Leading the melody
It kept at bay,
It was independent, rattling, non-transcendent
Ulster – old decency

And Old Bushmills,
Soda farls, strong tea,
New rope, rock salt, kale plants,
Potato-bread and Woodbine.
Wind through the concrete vents
Of a border check-point.
Cold zinc nailed for a peace line.

Fifteen years ago, come this October,
Crowded on your floor,
I got my arm round Marie's shoulder
For the first time.
'Oh, Sir Jasper, do not touch me!'
You roared across at me,
Chorus-leading, splashing out the wine.

The Otter

When you plunged
The light of Tuscany wavered
And swung through the pool
From top to bottom.

I loved your wet head and smashing crawl,
Your fine swimmer's back and shoulders
Surfacing and surfacing again
This year and every year since.

I sat dry-throated on the warm stones.
You were beyond me.
The mellowed clarities, the grape-deep air
Thinned and disappointed.

Thank God for the slow loadening,
When I hold you now
We are close and deep
As the atmosphere on water.

My two hands are plumbed water.
You are my palpable, lithe
Otter of memory
In the pool of the moment,

Turning to swim on your back,
Each silent, thigh-shaking kick
Re-tilting the light,
Heaving the cool at your neck.

And suddenly you're out,
Back again, intent as ever,
Heavy and frisky in your freshened pelt,
Printing the stones.

The Skunk

Up, black, striped and damasked like the chasuble
At a funeral mass, the skunk's tail
Paraded the skunk. Night after night
I expected her like a visitor.

The refrigerator whinnied into silence.
My desk light softened beyond the verandah.
Small oranges loomed in the orange tree.
I began to be tense as a voyeur.

After eleven years I was composing
Love-letters again, broaching the word 'wife'
Like a stored cask, as if its slender vowel
Had mutated into the night earth and air

Of California. The beautiful, useless
Tang of eucalyptus spelt your absence.
The aftermath of a mouthful of wine
Was like inhaling you off a cold pillow.

And there she was, the intent and glamorous,
Ordinary, mysterious skunk,
Mythologized, demythologized,
Snuffing the boards five feet beyond me.

It all came back to me last night, stirred
By the sootfall of your things at bedtime,
Your head-down, tail-up hunt in a bottom drawer
For the black plunge-line nightdress.

A Dream of Jealousy

Walking with you and another lady
In wooded parkland, the whispering grass
Ran its fingers through our guessing silence
And the trees opened into a shady
Unexpected clearing where we sat down.
I think the candour of the light dismayed us.
We talked about desire and being jealous,
Our conversation a loose single gown
Or a white picnic tablecloth spread out
Like a book of manners in the wilderness.
'Show me,' I said to our companion, 'what
I have much coveted, your breast's mauve star.'
And she consented. O neither these verses
Nor my prudence, love, can heal your wounded stare.

Field Work

I

Where the sally tree went pale in every breeze,
where the perfect eye of the nesting blackbird watched,
where one fern was always green

I was standing watching you
take the pad from the gatehouse at the crossing
and reach to lift a white wash off the whins.

I could see the vaccination mark
stretched on your upper arm, and smell the coal smell
of the train that comes between us, a slow goods,

waggon after waggon full of big-eyed cattle.

II

But your vaccination mark is on your thigh,
an O that's healed into the bark.

Except a dryad's not a woman
you are my wounded dryad

in a mothering smell of wet
and ring-wormed chestnuts.

Our moon was small and far,
was a coin long gazed at

brilliant on the *Pequod*'s mast
across Atlantic and Pacific waters.

III

Not the mud slick,
not the black weedy water
full of alder cones and pock-marked leaves.

Not the cow parsley in winter
with its old whitened shins and wrists,
its sibilance, its shaking.

Not even the tart green shade of summer
thick with butterflies
and fungus plump as a leather saddle.

No. But in a still corner,
braced to its pebble-dashed wall,
heavy, earth-drawn, all mouth and eye,

the sunflower, dreaming umber.

IV

Catspiss smell,
the pink bloom open:
I press a leaf
of the flowering currant
on the back of your hand
for the tight slow burn
of its sticky juice
to prime your skin,
and your veins to be crossed
criss-cross with leaf-veins.
I lick my thumb
and dip it in mould,
I anoint the anointed
leaf-shape. Mould
blooms and pigments
the back of the hand
like a birthmark –
my umber one,
you are stained, stained
to perfection.

The Harvest Bow

As you plaited the harvest bow
You implicated the mellowed silence in you
In wheat that does not rust
But brightens as it tightens twist by twist
Into a knowable corona,
A throwaway love-knot of straw.

Hands that aged round ashplants and cane sticks
And lapped the spurs on a lifetime of game cocks
Harked to their gift and worked with fine intent
Until your fingers moved somnambulant:
I tell and finger it like braille,
Gleaning the unsaid off the palpable,

And if I spy into its golden loops
I see us walk between the railway slopes
Into an evening of long grass and midges,
Blue smoke straight up, old beds and ploughs in hedges,
An auction notice on an outhouse wall –
You with a harvest bow in your lapel,

Me with the fishing rod, already homesick
For the big lift of these evenings, as your stick
Whacking the tips off weeds and bushes
Beats out of time, and beats, but flushes
Nothing: that original townland
Still tongue-tied in the straw tied by your hand.

The end of art is peace
Could be the motto of this frail device
That I have pinned up on our deal dresser –
Like a drawn snare
Slipped lately by the spirit of the corn
Yet burnished by its passage, and still warm.

In Memoriam Francis Ledwidge

Killed in France 31 July 1917

The bronze soldier hitches a bronze cape
That crumples stiffly in imagined wind
No matter how the real winds buff and sweep
His sudden hunkering run, forever craned

Over Flanders. Helmet and haversack,
The gun's firm slope from butt to bayonet,
The loyal, fallen names on the embossed plaque –
It all meant little to the worried pet

I was in nineteen forty-six or seven,
Gripping my Aunt Mary by the hand
Along the Portstewart prom, then round the crescent
To thread the Castle Walk out to the strand.

The pilot from Coleraine sailed to the coal-boat.
Courting couples rose out of the scooped dunes.
A farmer stripped to his studs and shiny waistcoat
Rolled the trousers down on his timid shins.

At night when coloured bulbs strung out the sea-front
Country voices rose from a cliff-top shelter
With news of a great litter – 'We'll pet the runt!' –
And barbed wire that had torn a friesian's elder.

Francis Ledwidge, you courted at the seaside
Beyond Drogheda one Sunday afternoon.
Literary, sweet-talking, countrified,
You pedalled out the leafy road from Slane

Where you belonged, among the dolorous
And lovely: the May altar of wild flowers,
Easter water sprinkled in outhouses,
Mass-rocks and hill-top raths and raftered byres.

I think of you in your Tommy's uniform,
A haunted Catholic face, pallid and brave,
Ghosting the trenches with a bloom of hawthorn
Or silence cored from a Boyne passage-grave.

It's summer, nineteen-fifteen. I see the girl
My aunt was then, herding on the long acre.
Behind a low bush in the Dardanelles
You suck stones to make your dry mouth water.

It's nineteen-seventeen. She still herds cows
But a big strafe puts the candles out in Ypres:
'My soul is by the Boyne, cutting new meadows . . .
My country wears her confirmation dress.'

'To be called a British soldier while my country
Has no place among nations . . .' You were rent
By shrapnel six weeks later. 'I am sorry
That party politics should divide our tents.'

In you, our dead enigma, all the strains
Criss-cross in useless equilibrium
And as the wind tunes through this vigilant bronze
I hear again the sure confusing drum

You followed from Boyne water to the Balkans
But miss the twilit note your flute should sound.
You were not keyed or pitched like these true-blue ones
Though all of you consort now underground.

Sloe Gin

The clear weather of juniper
darkened into winter.
She fed gin to sloes
and sealed the glass container.

When I unscrewed it
I smelled the disturbed
tart stillness of a bush
rising through the pantry.

When I poured it
it had a cutting edge
and flamed
like Betelgeuse.

I drink to you
in smoke-mirled, blue-black,
polished sloes, bitter
and dependable.

The Birthplace

I

The deal table where he wrote, so small and plain,
the single bed a dream of discipline.
And a flagged kitchen downstairs, its mote-slants

of thick light: the unperturbed, reliable
ghost life he carried, with no need to invent.
And high trees round the house, breathed upon

day and night by winds as slow as a cart
coming late from market, or the stir
a fiddle could make in his reluctant heart.

II

That day, we were like one
of his troubled pairs, speechless
until he spoke for them,

haunters of silence at noon
in a deep lane that was sexual
with ferns and butterflies,

scared at our hurt,
throat-sick, heat-struck, driven
into the damp-floored wood

where we made an episode
of ourselves, unforgettable,
unmentionable,

and broke out again like cattle
through bushes, wet and raised,
only yards from the house.

III

Everywhere being nowhere,
who can prove
one place more than another?

We come back emptied,
to nourish and resist
the words of coming to rest:

birthplace, roofbeam, whitewash,
flagstone, hearth,
like unstacked iron weights

afloat among galaxies.
Still, was it thirty years ago
I read until first light

for the first time, to finish
The Return of the Native?
The corncrake in the aftergrass

verified himself, and I heard
roosters and dogs, the very same
as if he had written them.

Changes

As you came with me in silence
to the pump in the long grass

I heard much that you could not hear:
the bite of the spade that sank it,

the slithering and grumble
as the mason mixed his mortar,

and women coming with white buckets
like flashes on their ruffled wings.

[267]

The cast-iron rims of the lid
clinked as I uncovered it,

something stirred in its mouth.
I had a bird's eye view of a bird,

finch-green, speckly white,
nesting on dry leaves, flattened, still,

suffering the light
So I roofed the citadel

as gently as I could, and told you
and you gently unroofed it

but where was the bird now?
There was a single egg, pebbly white,

and in the rusted bend of the spout
tail feathers splayed and sat tight.

So tender, I said, 'Remember this.
It will be good for you to retrace this path

when you have grown away and stand at last
at the very centre of the empty city.'

A Hazel Stick for Catherine Ann

The living mother-of-pearl of a salmon
just out of the water

is gone just like that, but your stick
is kept salmon-silver.

Seasoned and bendy,
it convinces the hand

that what you have you hold
to play with and pose with

and lay about with.
But then too it points back to cattle

and spatter and beating
the bars of a gate –

the very stick we might cut
from your family tree.

The living cobalt of an afternoon
dragonfly drew my eye to it first

and the evening I trimmed it for you
you saw your first glow-worm –

all of us stood round in silence, even you
gigantic enough to darken the sky

for a glow-worm.
And when I poked open the grass

a tiny brightening den lit the eye
in the blunt cut end of your stick.

Widgeon

for Paul Muldoon

It had been badly shot.
While he was plucking it
he found, he says, the voice box –

like a flute stop
in the broken windpipe –

and blew upon it
unexpectedly
his own small widgeon cries.

from Station Island

VII

I had come to the edge of the water,
soothed by just looking, idling over it
as if it were a clear barometer

or a mirror, when his reflection
did not appear but I sensed a presence
entering into my concentration

on not being concentrated as he spoke
my name. And though I was reluctant
I turned to meet his face and the shock

is still in me at what I saw. His brow
was blown open above the eye and blood
had dried on his neck and cheek. 'Easy now,'

he said, 'it's only me. You've seen men as raw
after a football match . . . What time it was
when I was wakened up I still don't know

but I heard this knocking, knocking, and it
scared me, like the phone in the small hours,
so I had the sense not to put on the light

but looked out from behind the curtain.
I saw two customers on the doorstep
and an old landrover with the doors open

[271]

parked on the street so I let the curtain drop;
but they must have been waiting for it to move
for they shouted to come down into the shop.

She started to cry then and roll round the bed,
lamenting and lamenting to herself,
not even asking who it was. "Is your head

astray, or what's come over you?" I roared, more
to bring myself to my senses
than out of any real anger at her

for the knocking shook me, the way they kept it up,
and her whingeing and half-screeching made it worse.
All the time they were shouting, "Shop!

Shop!" so I pulled on my shoes and a sportscoat
and went back to the window and called out,
"What do you want? Could you quieten the racket

or I'll not come down at all." "There's a child not well.
Open up and see what you have got – pills
or a powder or something in a bottle,"

one of them said. He stepped back off the footpath
so I could see his face in the street lamp
and when the other moved I knew them both.

But bad and all as the knocking was, the quiet
hit me worse. She was quiet herself now,
lying dead still, whispering to watch out.

At the bedroom door I switched on the light.
"It's odd they didn't look for a chemist.
Who are they anyway at this time of the night?"

she asked me, with the eyes standing in her head.
"I know them to see," I said, but something
made me reach and squeeze her hand across the bed

before I went downstairs into the aisle
of the shop. I stood there, going weak
in the legs. I remember the stale smell

of cooked meat or something coming through
as I went to open up. From then on
you know as much about it as I do.'

'Did they say nothing?' 'Nothing. What would they say?'
'Were they in uniform? Not masked in any way?'
'They were barefaced as they would be in the day,

shites thinking they were the be-all and the end-all.'
'Not that it is any consolation,
but they were caught,' I told him, 'and got jail.'

Big-limbed, decent, open-faced, he stood
forgetful of everything now except
whatever was welling up in his spoiled head,

beginning to smile. 'You've put on weight
since you did your courting in that big Austin
you got the loan of on a Sunday night.'

Through life and death he had hardly aged.
There always was an athlete's cleanliness
shining off him and except for the ravaged

forehead and the blood, he was still that same
rangy midfielder in a blue jersey
and starched pants, the one stylist on the team,

the perfect, clean, unthinkable victim.
'Forgive the way I have lived indifferent –
forgive my timid circumspect involvement,'

I surprised myself by saying. 'Forgive
my eye,' he said, 'all that's above my head.'
And then a stun of pain seemed to go through him

and he trembled like a heatwave and faded.

DEREK MAHON 1941–

Glengormley

'Wonders are many and none is more wonderful than man'
Who has tamed the terrier, trimmed the hedge
And grasped the principle of the watering-can.
Clothes-pegs litter the window ledge
And the long ships lie in clover. Washing lines
Shake out white linen over the chalk thanes.

Now we are safe from monsters, and the giants
Who tore up sods twelve miles by six
And hurled them out to sea to become islands
Can worry us no more. The sticks
And stones that once broke bones will not now harm
A generation of such sense and charm.

Only words hurt us now. No saint or hero,
Landing at night from the conspiring seas,
Brings dangerous tokens to the new era –
Their sad names linger in the histories.
The unreconciled, in their metaphysical pain,
Dangle from lamp-posts in the dawn rain;

And much dies with them. I should rather praise
A worldly time under this worldly sky –
The terrier-taming, garden-watering days
Those heroes pictured as they struggled through
The quick noose of their finite being. By
Necessity, if not choice, I live here too.

The Poets of the Nineties

Slowly, with the important carelessness
Of your kind, each spirit-sculptured face
Appears before me, eyes
Bleak from discoveries.

I had almost forgotten you had been,
So jealous was I of my skin
And the world with me. How
Goes it with you now?

Did death and its transitions disappoint you,
And the worms you so looked forward to?
Perhaps you found that you had to *queue*
For a ticket into hell,
Despite your sprays of laurel.

You were all children in your helpless wisdom,
Retiring loud-mouths who would not be dumb –
Frustrated rural clergymen
Nobody would ordain.

Then ask no favour of reincarnation,
No yearning after the booze and whores –
For you, if anyone,
Have played your part
In holding nature up to art . . .

Be content to sprawl in your upland meadows,
Hair and boy-mouths stuck with flowers –
And rest assured, the day
Will be all sunlight, and the night
A dutiful spectrum of stars.

In Carrowdore Churchyard

at the grave of Louis MacNeice

Your ashes will not stir, even on this high ground,
However the wind tugs, the headstones shake.
This plot is consecrated, for your sake,
To what lies in the future tense. You lie
Past tension now, and spring is coming round
Igniting flowers on the peninsula.

Your ashes will not fly, however the rough winds burst
Through the wild brambles and the reticent trees.
All we may ask of you we have. The rest
Is not for publication, will not be heard.
Maguire, I believe, suggested a blackbird
And over your grave a phrase from Euripides.

Which suits you down to the ground, like this churchyard
With its play of shadow, its humane perspective.
Locked in the winter's fist, these hills are hard
As nails, yet soft and feminine in their turn
When fingers open and the hedges burn.
This, you implied, is how we ought to live –

The ironical, loving crush of roses against snow,
Each fragile, solving ambiguity. So
From the pneumonia of the ditch, from the ague
Of the blind poet and the bombed-out town you bring
The all-clear to the empty holes of spring;
Rinsing the choked mud, keeping the colours new.

The Spring Vacation

for Michael Longley

Walking among my own this windy morning
In a tide of sunlight between shower and shower,
I resume my old conspiracy with the wet
Stone and the unwieldy images of the squinting heart.
Once more, as before, I remember not to forget.

There is a perverse pride in being on the side
Of the fallen angels and refusing to get up.
We could *all* be saved by keeping an eye on the hill
At the top of every street, for there it is,
Eternally, if irrelevantly, visible –

But yield instead to the humorous formulae,
The hidden menace in the knowing nod.
Or we keep sullen silence in light and shade,
Rehearsing our astute salvations under
The cold gaze of a sanctimonious God.

One part of my mind must learn to know its place.
The things that happen in the kitchen houses
And echoing back-streets of this desperate city
Should engage more than my casual interest,
Exact more interest than my casual pity.

Grandfather

They brought him in on a stretcher from the world,
Wounded but humorous. And he soon recovered.
Boiler-rooms, row upon row of gantries rolled
Away to reveal the landscape of a childhood
Only he can recapture. Even on cold
Mornings he is up at six with a block of wood
Or a box of nails, discreetly up to no good
Or banging round the house like a four-year-old –

Never there when you call. But after dark
You hear his great boots thumping in the hall
And in he comes, as cute as they come. Each night
His shrewd eyes bolt the door and set the clock
Against the future, then his light goes out.
Nothing escapes him; he escapes us all.

My Wicked Uncle

His was the first corpse I had ever seen,
Untypically silent in the front room.
Death had deprived him of his moustache,
His thick horn-rimmed spectacles,
The easy corners of his salesman dash –
Those things by which I had remembered him –
And sundered him behind a sort of gauze.
His hair was badly parted on the right
As if for Sunday School. That night
I saw my uncle as he really was.

The stories he retailed were mostly
Wicked-avuncular fantasy;
He went in for waistcoats and Brylcreem.
But something about him
Demanded that you picture the surprise
Of the Chairman of the Board, when to
'What will you have with your whiskey?' my uncle replies,
'Another whiskey please.'

He claimed to have been arrested in New York
Twice on the same day –
The crookedest chief steward in the Head Line.
And once, so he would say,
Sailing from San Francisco to Shanghai,
He brought a crew of lascars out on strike
In protest at the loss of a day's pay
Crossing the International Dateline.

He was buried on a blustery day above the sea,
The young Presbyterian minister
Tangled and wind-swept in the sea air.
I saw sheep huddled in the long wet grass
Of the golf course, and the empty freighters
Sailing for ever down Belfast Lough
In a fine rain, their sirens going,
As the gradual graph of my uncle's life
And times dipped precipitately
Into the black earth of Carnmoney Cemetery.

His teenage kids are growing horns and claws –
More wicked already than ever my uncle was.

An Unborn Child

I have already come to the verge of
Departure. A month or so and
I shall be vacating this familiar room.
Its fabric fits me like a glove
While leaving latitude for a free hand.
I begin to put on the manners of the world,
Sensing the splitting light above
My head, where in the silence I lie curled.

Certain mysteries are relayed to me
Through the dark network of my mother's body
While she sits sewing the white shrouds
Of my apotheosis. I know the twisted
Kitten that lies there sunning itself
Under the bare bulb, the clouds
Of goldfish mooning around upon the shelf.
In me these data are already vested;

I feel them in my bones – bones which embrace
Nothing, for I am completely egocentric.
The pandemonium of encumbrances
Which will absorb me, mind and senses –
Intricacies of the box and the rat-race –
I imagine only. Though they linger and,
Like fingers, stretch until the knuckles crack,
They cannot dwarf the dimensions of my hand.

I must compose myself in the nerve-centre
Of this metropolis, and not fidget –
Although sometimes at night, when the city
Has gone to sleep, I keep in touch with it,
Listening to the warm red water
Racing in the sewers of my mother's body;
Or the moths, soft as eyelids, or the rain
Wiping its wet wings on the window-pane.

And sometimes too, in the small hours of the morning
When the dead filament has ceased to ring,
After the goldfish are dissolved in darkness
And the kitten has gathered itself up into a ball
Between the groceries and the sewing,
I slip the trappings of my harness
To range these hollows in discreet rehearsal
And, battering at the concavity of my caul,

Produce in my mouth the words 'I want to live!' –
This my first protest, and shall be my last.
As I am innocent, everything I do
Or say is couched in the affirmative.
I want to see, hear, touch and taste
These things with which I am to be encumbered.
Perhaps I needn't worry. Give
Or take a day or two, my days are numbered.

The Studio

You would think with so much going on outside
The deal table would make for the window,
The ranged crockery freak and wail
Remembering its dark origins, the frail
Oilcloth, in a fury of recognitions,
Disperse in a thousand directions,
And the simple bulb in the ceiling, honed
By death to a worm of pain, to a hair
Of heat, to a light snowflake laid

In a dark river at night – and wearied
Above all by the life-price of time
And the failure by only a few tenths
Of an inch but completely and for ever
Of the ends of a carefully drawn equator
To meet, sing and be one – abruptly
Roar into the floor.
              But it
Never happens like that. Instead
There is this quivering silence
In which, day by day, the play
Of light and shadow (shadow mostly)
Repeats itself, though never exactly.

This is the all-purpose bed-, work- and bedroom.
Its mourning faces are cracked porcelain only quicker,
Its knuckles door-knobs only lighter,
Its occasional cries of despair
A function of the furniture.

Lives

for Seamus Heaney

First time out
I was a torc of gold
And wept tears of the sun.

That was fun
But they buried me
In the earth two thousand years

Till a labourer
Turned me up with a pick
In eighteen fifty-four

And sold me
For tea and sugar
In Newmarket-on-Fergus.

Once I was an oar
But stuck in the shore
To mark the place of a grave

When the lost ship
Sailed away. I thought
Of Ithaca, but soon decayed.

The time that I liked
Best was when
I was a bump of clay

In a Navaho rug,
Put there to mitigate
The too godlike

Perfection of that
Merely human artifact.
I served my maker well –

He lived long
To be struck down in
Tucson by an electric shock

The night the lights
Went out in Europe
Never to shine again.

So many lives,
So many things to remember!
I was a stone in Tibet,

A tongue of bark
At the heart of Africa
Growing darker and darker . . .

It all seems
A little unreal now,
Now that I am

An anthropologist
With my own
Credit card, dictaphone,

Army surplus boots,
And a whole boatload
Of photographic equipment.

I know too much
To be anything any more;
And if in the distant

Future someone
Thinks he has once been me
As I am today,

Let him revise
His insolent ontology
Or teach himself to pray.

Poem Beginning with a Line by Cavafy

It is night and the barbarians have not come.
It was not always so hard;
When the great court flared
With gallowglasses and language difficulty
A man could be a wheelwright and die happy.

We remember oatmeal and mutton,
Harpsong, a fern table for
Wiping your hands on,
A candle of reeds and butter,
The distaste of the rheumatic chronicler,

A barbarous tongue, and herds like cloud-shadow
Roaming the wet hills
When the hills were young,
Whiskery pikemen and their spiky dogs
Preserved in woodcuts and card-catalogues.

Now it is night and the barbarians have not come.
Or if they have we only recognize,
Harsh as a bombed bathroom,
The frantic anthropologisms
And lazarous ironies behind their talk

Of fitted carpets, central heating
And automatic gear-change –
Like the bleached bones of a hare
Or a handful of spent
Cartridges on a deserted rifle range.

Father-in-Law

While your widow clatters water into a kettle
You lie at peace in your southern grave –
A sea captain who died at sea, almost.
Lost voyager, what would you think of me,
Husband of your fair daughter but impractical?
You stare from the mantelpiece, a curious ghost
In your peaked cap, as we sit down to tea.
The bungalows still signal to the sea,
Rain wanders the golf course as in your day,
The river flows past the distillery
And a watery sun shines on Portballintrae.

I think we would have had a lot in common –
Alcohol and the love of one woman
Certainly; but I failed the eyesight test
When I tried for the Merchant Navy,
And lapsed into this lyric lunacy.
When you lost your balance like Li Po
They found unfinished poems in your sea-chest.

Homage to Malcolm Lowry

For gear your typewriter and an old rugby boot,
The voyage started, clearly, when you were born
That danced those empty bottles. When you set out
On a round-the-cosmos trip with the furious Muse
Or lay sweating on a hotel bed in Vera Cruz,
Did you not think you had left that pool astern
Where a soul might bathe and be clean or slake its drought?
In any case, your deportment in those seas
Was faultless. Lightning-blind, you, tempest-torn
At the poles of our condition, did not confuse
The Gates of Ivory with the Gates of Horn.

The Snow Party

for Louis Asekoff

Bashō, coming
To the city of Nagoya,
Is asked to a snow party.

There is a tinkling of china
And tea into china;
There are introductions.

[291]

Then everyone
Crowds to the window
To watch the falling snow.

Snow is falling on Nagoya
And farther south
On the tiles of Kyōto.

Eastward, beyond Irago,
It is falling
Like leaves on the cold sea.

Elsewhere they are burning
Witches and heretics
In the boiling squares,

Thousands have died since dawn
In the service
Of barbarous kings;

But there is silence
In the houses of Nagoya
And the hills of Ise.

DEREK MAHON

The Last of the Fire Kings

I want to be
Like the man who descends
At two milk churns

With a bulging
String bag and vanishes
Where the lane turns,

Or the man
Who drops at night
From a moving train

And strikes out over the fields
Where fireflies glow
Not knowing a word of the language.

Either way, I am
Through with history –
Who lives by the sword

Dies by the sword.
Last of the fire kings, I shall
Break with tradition and

Die by my own hand
Rather than perpetuate
The barbarous cycle.

Five years I have reigned
During which-time
I have lain awake each night

And prowled by day
In the sacred grove
For fear of the usurper,

Perfecting my cold dream
Of a place out of time,
A palace of porcelain

Where the frugivorous
Inheritors recline
In their rich fabrics
Far from the sea.

But the fire-loving
People, rightly perhaps,
Will not countenance this,

Demanding that I inhabit,
Like them, a world of
Sirens, bin-lids
And bricked-up windows –

Not to release them
From the ancient curse
But to die their creature and be thankful.

Nostalgias

The chair squeaks in a high wind,
Rain falls from its branches,
The kettle yearns for the
Mountain, the soap for the sea.
In a tiny stone church
On the desolate headland
A lost tribe is singing 'Abide With Me'.

The Mute Phenomena

after Nerval

Your great mistake is to disregard the satire
Bandied among the mute phenomena.
Be strong if you must, your brusque hegemony
Means fuck-all to the somnolent sunflower
Or the extinct volcano. What do you know
Of the revolutionary theories advanced
By turnips, or the sex-life of cutlery?
Everything is susceptible, Pythagoras said so.

An ordinary common-or-garden brick wall, the kind
For talking to or banging your head on,
Resents your politics and bad draughtsmanship.
God is alive and lives under a stone.
Already in a lost hub-cap is conceived
The ideal society which will replace our own.

A Disused Shed in Co. Wexford

Let them not forget us, the weak souls among the asphodels.
– Seferis, *Mythistorema*

for J. G. Farrell

Even now there are places where a thought might grow –
Peruvian mines, worked out and abandoned
To a slow clock of condensation,
An echo trapped for ever, and a flutter
Of wildflowers in the lift-shaft,
Indian compounds where the wind dances
And a door bangs with diminished confidence,
Lime crevices behind rippling rainbarrels,
Dog corners for bone burials;
And in a disused shed in Co. Wexford,

Deep in the grounds of a burnt-out hotel,
Among the bathtubs and the washbasins
A thousand mushrooms crowd to a keyhole.
This is the one star in their firmament
Or frames a star within a star.
What should they do there but desire?
So many days beyond the rhododendrons
With the world waltzing in its bowl of cloud,
They have learnt patience and silence
Listening to the rooks querulous in the high wood.

They have been waiting for us in a foetor
Of vegetable sweat since civil war days,
Since the gravel-crunching, interminable departure
Of the expropriated mycologist.
He never came back, and light since then
Is a keyhole rusting gently after rain.
Spiders have spun, flies dusted to mildew
And once a day, perhaps, they have heard something –
A trickle of masonry, a shout from the blue
Or a lorry changing gear at the end of the lane.

There have been deaths, the pale flesh flaking
Into the earth that nourished it;
And nightmares, born of these and the grim
Dominion of stale air and rank moisture.
Those nearest the door grow strong –
'Elbow room! Elbow room!'
The rest, dim in a twilight of crumbling
Utensils and broken flower-pots, groaning
For their deliverance, have been so long
Expectant that there is left only the posture.

A half century, without visitors, in the dark –
Poor preparation for the cracking lock
And creak of hinges. Magi, moonmen,
Powdery prisoners of the old regime,
Web-throated, stalked like triffids, racked by drought
And insomnia, only the ghost of a scream
At the flash-bulb firing squad we wake them with
Shows there is life yet in their feverish forms.
Grown beyond nature now, soft food for worms,
They lift frail heads in gravity and good faith.

They are begging us, you see, in their wordless way,
To do something, to speak on their behalf
Or at least not to close the door again.
Lost people of Treblinka and Pompeii!
'Save us, save us,' they seem to say,
'Let the god not abandon us
Who have come so far in darkness and in pain.
We too had our lives to live.
You with your light meter and relaxed itinerary,
Let not our naive labours have been in vain!'

Autobiographies

for Maurice Leitch

1.   *The Home Front*

While the frozen armies trembled
At the gates of Stalingrad
They took me home in a taxi
And laid me in my cot,
And there I slept again
With siren and black-out;

And slept under the stairs
Beside the light meter
When bombs fell on the city;
So I never saw the sky
Filled with a fiery glow,
Searchlights roaming the stars.

But I do remember one time
(I must have been four then)
Being held up to the window
For a victory parade –
Soldiers, sailors and airmen
Lining the Antrim Road;

And, later, hide-and-seek
Among the air-raid shelters,
The last ration coupons,
Oranges and bananas,
Forage caps and badges
And packets of Lucky Strike.

Gracie Fields on the radio!
Americans in the art-deco
Milk bars! The released Jews
Blinking in shocked sunlight . . .
A male child in a garden
Clutching *The Empire News*.

2. *The Lost Girls*

'In ancient shadows and twilights
Where childhood had strayed'
I ran round in the playground
Of Skegoneill Primary School
During the lunch hour,
Pretending to be a plane.

For months I would dawdle home
At a respectful distance
Behind the teacher's daughter,
Eileen Boyd, who lived
In a house whose back garden
Was visible from my window.

I watched her on summer evenings,
A white dress picking flowers,
Her light, graceful figure
Luminous and remote.
We never exchanged greetings:
Her house was bigger than ours.

She married an older man
And went to live in Kenya.
Perhaps she is there still
Complaining about 'the natives'.
It would be nice to know;
But who can re-live their lives?

Eileen Boyd, Hazel and Heather
Thompson, Patricia King –
The lost girls in a ring
On a shadowy school playground
Like the nymphs dancing together
In the 'Allegory of Spring'.

DEREK MAHON

Courtyards in Delft

Pieter de Hooch, 1659

for Gordon Woods

Oblique light on the trite, on brick and tile –
Immaculate masonry, and everywhere that
Water tap, that broom and wooden pail
To keep it so. House-proud, the wives
Of artisans pursue their thrifty lives
Among scrubbed yards, modest but adequate.
Foliage is sparse, and clings. No breeze
Ruffles the trim composure of those trees.

No spinet-playing emblematic of
The harmonies and disharmonies of love;
No lewd fish, no fruit, no wide-eyed bird
About to fly its cage while a virgin
Listens to her seducer, mars the chaste
Precision of the thing and the thing made.
Nothing is random, nothing goes to waste:
We miss the dirty dog, the fiery gin.

That girl with her back to us who waits
For her man to come home for his tea
Will wait till the paint disintegrates
And ruined dykes admit the esurient sea;
Yet this is life too, and the cracked
Out-house door a verifiable fact
As vividly mnemonic as the sunlit
Railings that front the houses opposite.

I lived there as a boy and know the coal
Glittering in its shed, late-afternoon
Lambency informing the deal table,
The ceiling cradled in a radiant spoon.
I must be lying low in a room there,
A strange child with a taste for verse,
While my hard-nosed companions dream of war
On parched veldt and fields of rain-swept gorse;

For the pale light of that provincial town
Will spread itself, like ink or oil,
Over the not yet accurate linen
Map of the world which occupies one wall
And punish nature in the name of God.
If only, now, the Maenads, as of right,
Came smashing crockery, with fire and sword,
We could sleep easier in our beds at night.

Tractatus

for Aidan Higgins

'The world is everything that is the case'
From the fly giving up in the coal-shed
To the Winged Victory of Samothrace.
Give blame, praise, to the fumbling God
Who hides, shame-facèdly, His agèd face;
Whose light retires behind its veil of cloud.

The world, though, is also so much more –
Everything that is the case imaginatively.
Tacitus believed mariners could *hear*
The sun sinking into the western sea;
And who would question that titanic roar,
The steam rising wherever the edge may be?

A Lighthouse in Maine

It might be anywhere,
That ivory tower
Approached by a dirt road.

Bleached stone against
Bleached sky, it faces
Every way with an air

Of squat omniscience –
A polished Buddha
Hard and bright beyond

Vegetable encroachment.
The north light
That strikes its frame

Houses is not
The light of heaven
But that of this world;

[303]

Nor is its task
To throw a punctual
Glow in the dark

To liners wild
With rock music and calm
With navigation.

Though built to shed
Light, it prefers
To shelter it, as it does

Now in the one-bird hour
Of afternoon, a milky
Glare melting the telephone poles.

It works both ways,
Of course, light
Being, like love and the cold,

Something that you
Can give and keep
At the same time.

Night and day it sits
Above the ocean like
A kindly eye, keeping

And giving the rainbow
Of its many colours,
Each of them white.

It might be anywhere –
Hokkaido, Normandy, Maine;
But it is in Maine.

You make a right
Somewhere beyond Rockland,
A left, a right,

You turn a corner and
There it is, shining
In modest glory like

The soul of Adonais.
Out you get and
Walk the rest of the way.

A Garage in Co. Cork

Surely you paused at this roadside oasis
In your nomadic youth, and saw the mound
Of never-used cement, the curious faces,
The soft-drink ads and the uneven ground
Rainbowed with oily puddles, where a snail
Had scrawled its slimy, phosphorescent trail.

Like a frontier store-front in an old western
It might have nothing behind it but thin air,
Building materials, fruit boxes, scrap iron,
Dust-laden shrubs and coils of rusty wire,
A cabbage-white fluttering in the sodden
Silence of an untended kitchen garden.

Nirvana! But the cracked panes reveal a dark
Interior echoing with the cries of children.
Here in this quiet corner of Co. Cork
A family ate, slept, and watched the rain
Dance clean and cobalt the exhausted grit
So that the mind shrank from the glare of it.

Where did they go? South Boston? Cricklewood?
Somebody somewhere thinks of this as home,
Remembering the old pumps where they stood,
Antique now, squirting juice into a chrome
Lagonda or a dung-caked tractor while
A cloud swam on a cloud-reflecting tile.

Surely a whitewashed sun-trap at the back
Gave way to hens, wild thyme, and the first few
Shadowy yards of an overgrown cart-track,
Tyres in the branches such as Noah knew –
Beyond, a swoop of mountain where you heard,
Disconsolate in the haze, a single blackbird.

Left to itself, the functional will cast
A death-bed glow of picturesque abandon.
The intact antiquities of the recent past,
Dropped from the retail catalogues, return
To the materials that gave rise to them
And shine with a late sacramental gleam.

A god who spent the night here once rewarded
Natural courtesy with eternal life –
Changing to petrol pumps, that they be spared
For ever there, an old man and his wife.
The virgin who escaped his dark design
Sanctions the townland from her prickly shrine.

We might be anywhere – in the Dordogne,
Iquitos, Bethlehem – wherever the force
Of gravity secures houses and the sun
Selects this fan-blade of the universe
Decelerating while the fates devise
What outcome for the dawdling galaxies?

But we are in one place and one place only,
One of the milestones of earth-residence
Unique in each particular, the thinly
Peopled hinterland serenely tense –
Not in the hope of a resplendent future
But with a sure sense of its intrinsic nature.

PAUL DURCAN 1944–

Letter to Ben, 1972

4 The Terrace, At The Ridge of The Two Air-Demons, Co. Leitrim

It is half-past nine on a July night;
The town's, and the emperor's, artillery are outside,
Are all perched up inside an ocean wave that's riding
– Alongwith the weed-adorned boards of sunlight, filthy
                              jewels and millefiori refuse –
Seabreezes that themselves are riding into each other at
                                             right angles
Across this broken street we call *The Terrace*;
And there is grass growing in the sand and old Ben
Is stretched out happily in a sunny corner too – never again
Will he or I be a cause of fright to each other;
We're on the same side, just different sides of the ocean.

Come on up, Ben, take a seat in the gods,
The roof has at least three-quarters blown off,
Even the grey pools by the bridge cannot help
But be motherfathers to wildflowers
And all the wild animals too, including ourselves, the bear
                                             and the fox,
Whom tycoons thought to cage,
Have broken grave and cursed no one:
We know the mines will produce in their own time
Abundance:
Iron hills in the east
And gold in the northwest.

Oh such light from the east, Ben,
And it is only half-past nine on a summer's night.
Darkness has entered already the arena
Trampling the manure-larded sand and straw
With all her young splendour more bare and ebony than
                                                    before;
Her ceremonial chains proclaiming no escape nor for the
                                                    spectator.
So, in history, the ridge becomes deserted now and then:
Right now, just you and me, Ben, and the species.

They Say the Butterfly is the Hardest Stroke

for Richard Riordan

From coves below the cliffs of the years
I have dipped into *Ulysses*,
A Vagrant, *Tarry Flynn* –
But for no more than ten minutes or a page;
For no more than to keep in touch
With minds kindred in their romance with silence.
I have not 'met' God, I have not 'read'
David Gascoyne, James Joyce, or Patrick Kavanagh:
I believe in them.
Of the song of him with the world in his care
I am content to know the air.

November 1967

to Katherine

I awoke with a pain in my head
And my mother standing at the end of the bed;
'There's bad news in the paper,' she said
'Patrick Kavanagh is dead.'

After a week which was not real
At last I settled down to a natural meal;
I was sitting over a pint and a beef sandwich
In Mooney's across the street from the Rotunda.

By accident I happened to tune in
To the conversation at the table from me;
I heard an old Northsider tell to his missus
'He was pure straight; God rest him; not like us.'

General Vallancey's Waltz

for A.K.

I'm a Westmeath solicitor long lost in Peking, long, lost,
                                        and forgotten,
And I used sit up in my hall late into the night listening for
                                                    you;

But it was not enough, it was not enough,
So I sailed up the Liffey from China,
Back to the wall, back to the wall,
To Liberty Hall.

I got married in due course, to a good Peking lass, of good
                                        Communist stock,
But she turned turkey on me, said she needed more
                                                    money,
That there was not enough, that there was not enough,
So I sailed up the Liffey from China,
Back to the wall, back to the wall,
To Liberty Hall.

Oh forgive me my shout if I fall through your easy chair,
                        through the back of your easy chair,
My knees are the crux of the world's local problem, no
                                        knees – no heaven;
Oh but there *is* all in all, there *is* all in all,
So I sailed up the Liffey from China,
Back to the wall, back to the wall,
To Liberty Hall.

Ireland 1972

Next to the fresh grave of my beloved grandmother
The grave of my firstlove murdered by my brother.

PAUL DURCAN

Combe Florey

to Laura Waugh

Wilderness that not always would deliver:
But to us come from the hot clink of London
It was Tel Aviv the hill of Spring and garden of the Sea
To wake in the mornings and to hear the stillness –
And that in spite or because of
The racket of birds – more than one
Woodpecker inhabited the oak outside my window
And at six each morning wound up their clocks in a loud
                                                        manner
Not to speak of the woodpigeon, the cuckoo, the others
Whose names I do not know.
I said to the woman of the house in my own painful and
                                              boulder fashion:
It is a crying shame to be a creature of this earth
And not know the names of the birds in the trees
And yet I know the names of fifty motor cars.
She said: Lord, I do not think I know the name of even one
                                              of the little creatures.
And so saying, she gave tiny feet back to my boulder and
                                                        pain.

Nessa

I met her on the First of August
In the Shangri-La Hotel,
She took me by the index finger
And dropped me in her well.
And that was a whirlpool, that was a whirlpool,
And I very nearly drowned.

Take off your pants, she said to me,
And I very nearly didn't;
Would you care to swim, she said to me,
And I hopped into the Irish sea.
And that was a whirlpool, that was a whirlpool,
And I very nearly drowned.

On the way back I fell in the field
And she fell down beside me.
I'd have lain in the grass with her all my life
With Nessa:
She was a whirlpool, she was a whirlpool,
And I very nearly drowned.

Oh Nessa my dear, Nessa my dear,
Will you stay with me on the rocks?
Will you come for me into the Irish sea
And for me let your red hair down?
And then we will ride into Dublin city
In a taxi-cab wrapped-up in dust.
Oh you are a whirlpool, you are a whirlpool,
And I am very nearly drowned.

In Memory of Those Murdered in the Dublin Massacre, May 1974

In the grime-ridden sunlight in the downtown Wimpy bar
I think of all the crucial aeons – and of the labels
That freedom fighters stick onto the lost destinies of
                                    unborn children;
The early morning sunlight carries in the whole street from
                                                    outside;
The whole wide street from outside through the plate-glass
                                                    windows;
Wholly, sparklingly, surgingly, carried in from outside;
And the waitresses cannot help but be happy and gay
As they swipe at the table-tops with their dishcloths –
Such a moment as would provide the heroic freedom fighter
With his perfect meat.
And I think of those heroes – heroes? – and how truly
Obscene is war.

And as I stand up to walk out –
The aproned old woman who's been sweeping the floor
Has mop stuck in bucket, leaning on it;
And she's trembling all over, like a flower in the breeze.
She'd make a mighty fine explosion now, if you were to
                                                blow her up;
An explosion of petals, of aeons, and the waitresses too,
                                    flying breasts and limbs,
For a free Ireland.

The Kilfenora Teaboy

I'm the Kilfenora teaboy
And I'm not so very young,
But though the land is going to pieces
I will not take up the gun;
I am happy making tea,
I make lots of it when I can,
And when I can't – I just make do;
And I do a small bit of sheepfarming on the side.

Oh but it's the small bit of furze between two towns
Is what makes the Kilfenora teaboy really run.

I have nine healthy daughters
And please God I will have more,
Sometimes my dear wife beats me
But on the whole she's a gentle soul;
When I'm not making her some tea
I sit out and watch them all
Ring-a-rosying in the street;
And I do a small bit of sheepfarming on the side.

Oh but it's the small bit of furze between two towns
Is what makes the Kilfenora teaboy really run.

Oh indeed my wife is handsome,
She has a fire lighting in each eye,
You can pluck laughter from her elbows
And from her knees pour money's tears;
I make all my tea for her,
I'm her teaboy on the hill,
And I also thatch her roof;
And I do a small bit of sheepfarming on the side.

Oh but it's the small bit of furze between two towns
Is what makes the Kilfenora teaboy really run.

And I'm not only a famous teaboy,
I'm a famous caveman too;
I paint pictures by the hundred
But you can't sell walls;
Although the people praise my pictures
As well as my turf-perfumed blend
They rarely fling a fiver in my face;
Oh don't we do an awful lot of dying on the side?

But Oh it's the small bit of furze between two towns
Is what makes the Kilfenora teaboy really run.

Ireland 1977

'I've become so lonely, I could die' – he writes,
The native who is an exile in his native land:
'Do you hear me whispering to you across the Golden Vale?
Do you hear me bawling to you across the hearthrug?'

Making Love outside Áras an Uachtaráin

When I was a boy, myself and my girl
Used bicycle up to the Phoenix Park;
Outside the gates we used lie in the grass
Making love outside Áras an Uachtaráin.

Often I wondered what de Valera would have thought
Inside in his ivory tower
If he knew that we were in his green, green grass
Making love outside Áras an Uachtaráin.

Because the odd thing was – oh how odd it was –
We both revered Irish patriots
And we dreamed our dreams of a green, green flag
Making love outside Áras an Uachtaráin.

But even had our names been Diarmaid and Gráinne
We doubted de Valera's approval
For a poet's son and a judge's daughter
Making love outside Áras an Uachtaráin.

I see him now in the heat-haze of the day
Blindly stalking us down;
And, levelling an ancient rifle, he says 'Stop
Making love outside Áras an Uachtaráin.'

Micheál Mac Liammóir

'Dear Boy, What a superlative day for a funeral:
It seems St Stephen's Green put on the appareil
Of early Spring-time especially for me.
That is no vanity: but – dare I say it – humility
In the fell face of those nay-neighers who say we die
At dying-time. Die? Why, I must needs cry
No, no, no, no,
Now I am living whereas before – no –
'Twas but breathing, choking, croaking, singing,
Superb sometimes but nevertheless but breathing:
You should have seen the scene in University Church:
Packed to the hammer-beams with me left in the lurch
All on my ownio up-front centre-stage;
People of every nationality in Ireland and of every age;
Old age and youth – Oh, everpresent, oldest, wished-for
                                                    youth;
And old Dublin ladies telling their beads for old me;
                                                    forsooth.
'Twould have fired the cockles of John Henry's heart
And his mussels too: only Sara Bernhardt
Was missing but I was so glad to see Marie Conmee
Fresh, as always, as the morning sea.
We paid a last farewell to dear Harcourt Terrace,
Dear old, bedraggled, doomed Harcourt Terrace
Where I enjoyed, amongst the crocuses, a Continual
                                        Glimpse of Heaven
By having, for a living partner, Hilton.
Around the corner the canal-waters from Athy gleamed
Engaged in their never-ending courtship of Ringsend.

Then onward to the Gate – and to the rose-cheeked ghost
                           of Lord Edward Longford;
I could not bear to look at Patrick Bedford.
Oh tears there were, there and everywhere,
But especially there; there outside the Gate where
For fifty years we wooed the goddess of our art;
How many, many nights she pierced my heart.
Ach, níl aon tinteán mar do thinteán féin:
The Gate and the *Taibhdhearc* – each was our name;
I dreamed a dream of Jean Cocteau
Leaning against a wall in Killnamoe;
And so I voyaged through all the nations of Ireland with
                                   McMaster
And played in Cinderella an ugly, but oh so ugly, sister.
Ah but we could not tarry for ever outside the Gate;
Life, as always, must go on or we'd be late
For my rendezvous with my brave grave-diggers
Who were as shy but snappy as my best of dressers.
We sped past the vast suburb of Clontarf – all those lives
Full of hard-working Brian Borús with their busy wives.
In St Fintan's Cemetery there was spray from the sea
As well as from the noonday sun, and clay on me:
And a green carnation on my lonely oaken coffin.
Lonely in heaven? Yes, I must not soften
The deep pain I feel at even a momentary separation
From my dear, sweet friends. A green carnation
For you all, dear boy; If you must weep, ba(w)ll;
Slán agus Beannacht: Micheál.'

Sally

Sally, I was happy with *you*.

Yet a dirty cafeteria in a railway station –
In the hour before dawn over a formica table
Confetti'ed with cigarette ash and coffee stains –
Was all we ever knew of a home together.

'Give me a child and let me go.'
'Give me a child and let me stay.'
She to him and he to her;
Which said *which*? and *who* was *who*?

Sally, I was happy with *you*.

TOM PAULIN   1949–

States

That stretch of water, it's always
There for you to cross over
To the other shore, observing
The lights of cities on blackness.

Your army jacket at the rail
Leaks its kapok into a wind
That slices gulls over a dark zero
Waste a cormorant skims through.

Any state, built on such a nature,
Is a metal convenience, its paint
Cheapened by the price of lives
Spent in a public service.

The men who peer out for dawning
Gantries below a basalt beak,
Think their vigils will make something
Clearer, as the cities close

With each other, their security
Threatened but bodied in steel
Polities that clock us safely
Over this dark; freighting us.

Settlers

They cross from Glasgow to a black city
   Of gantries, mills and steeples. They begin to belong.
He manages the Iceworks, is an elder of the Kirk;
   She becomes, briefly, a cook in Carson's Army.
Some mornings, walking through the company gate,
   He touches the bonnet of a brown lorry.
It is warm. The men watch and say nothing.
   'Queer, how it runs off in the night,'
He says to McCullough, then climbs to his office.
   He stores a warm knowledge on his palm.

   Nightlandings on the Antrim coast, the movement of
                          guns
Now snug in their oiled paper below the floors
   Of sundry kirks and tabernacles in that county.

Thinking of Iceland

     Forgetting the second cod war
     to go North to that island
     that's four days' sailing from Hull
     would be what? An escape?
     Or an attempt at finding
     what's behind everything?
     (Too big the last question for a holiday trip.)

Still, reading the letters
they fired back to England
(one, unfortunately, to Crossman)
brings back a winter monochrome
of coast and small townships
that are much nearer home:
Doochery, the Rosses, Bloody Foreland.

An empty road over hills
dips under some wind-bent,
scrub trees, there's a bar
painted pink, some houses,
a petrol pump by a shop;
it's permanently out-of-season
here where some people live for some reason.

A cluster too small for a village,
fields waste with grey rocks
that lichens coat – hard skin
spread like frozen cultures,
green, corroded tufts that make dyes
for tweed – shuttles clack
in draughty cottages based in this sour outback.

On the signposts every place
has two names; people live
in a cold climate, a landscape
whose silence denies efforts
no one feels much like making:
when someone is building
it looks like a joke, as though they're having us on.

[329]

They poke laughing faces
through fresh wooden struts and throw
a greeting from new rafters;
on the box in the bar
a sponsored programme begins;
the crime rate is low – small sins
like poaching or drink. It's far to the border.

Now that a small factory
which cans and dries vegetables
has opened, some girls stay
and scour the county for dances.
In these bleak parishes that seem
dissolved in a grey dream
some men are busy mixing concrete, digging septics.

In winter there is work
with the council on the roads,
or with local contractors.
Each year Packy Harkin
builds a new boat, choosing
for a keel a long curving
branch from a sheltered wood where oaks grow straight.

In the dark panelled bar
through the shop, there's a faded
print of an eviction:
one constable crouches
on the thatch, the family stands
at the door, pale, while bands
of constabulary guard the whiskered bailiff.

In the top corner, clumsily,
the face of a young woman
glimmers: *The Irish patriot,*
Miss Maud Gonne. Sour smell of porter,
clutter of hens in the yard:
no docking in sagaland –
the wish got as far as this coast, then worked inland.

And yet, at Holar, striking matches
in church, trying to snap
a carved altar piece: strange figures
absent-mindedly slaughtering
prisoners; or 'exchanging politenesses'
with Goering's brother at breakfast,
was this coming-full-circle not the question they asked?

From

You've made a table you say, and are happy.
It's easy to understand where you are.
I can see you in a room we both know,
Cutting fresh wood, looking up now and then
To a window autumn light comes through.
There is a green glass float on the sill
And two stone jars we found washed by storms
On the strand. In the blueness outside, frost
And a light that, touching, makes what you see.
In that still light and silence the long hills
That ring the bay are brittle, fixed in glaze.

[331]

The island below you is a lost place
That no one can cross to in the neap,
The winter season. The tides slack,
But they never pull back; the graveyard
And ruined chapel are not to be reached now.
A priest lived there in the house when processions
Used to cross the sands slowly, in black.
Rotting boards nailed to its windows, that hermitage
Is obsolete. The light stays at that end
Of the island, catches that small, broken settlement
Where thin stones, laid flat on a humped ground,
Are carved with turnip skulls and crude bones.
A soft grass covers them and light falls.

Inishkeel Parish Church

Standing at the gate before the service started,
In their Sunday suits, the Barrets talked together,
Smiled shyly at the visitors who packed the church
In summer. A passing congregation
Who mostly knew each other, were sometimes fashionable,
Their sons at prep school, the daughters boarding.
Inside it was as neat and tight as a boat.
Stone flags and whitewashed walls, a little brass.
Old Mrs Flewitt played the organ and Mr Alwell
Read the lessons in an accent as sharp as salt.

O Absalom, Absalom, my son,
An hour is too long, there are too many people,
Too many heads and eyes and thoughts that clutter.

Only one moment counted with the lessons
And that was when, the pressure just too much,
You walked slowly out of that packed church
Into bright cold air.
Then, before the recognitions and the talk,
There was an enormous sight of the sea,
A silent water beyond society.

Cadaver Politic

The grey hills of that country fall away
  Like folds of skin. There are some mountains somewhere
And public parks with metal fountains.
  Rains fall and then fogs freeze, drifting
Over empty stretches of water, forts
  With broken walls on small islands.
Rafted cities smoke in the rain and sharp posts
  Have been knocked deep into flabby ground,
Thin tatters of chicken wire strung to them.
  Coffins are moored in its bays and harbours.
A damp rag, it flies several flags –
  Bunting and boneyard streamers, the badges
Of territory. In the waste, silent valleys
  Clans are at their manœuvres.
At the bottom of a cliff, on a tussock
  Of ground by a lean-to shed, a group
Of men and women huddle, watching a man
  Who tries, with damp matches, to light a board
Washed on that coast by the grey sea.

[333]

The Hyperboreans

Those city states staked out
On flat, thousand-acre sites
Of damp moorland
Are the theoretical locations
Most of us inhabit.

The iron-bound, leather volumes
Of political philosophies
Silting the dust
In brown country-house libraries
Are fulfilled here

(Just turning a tap on proves it).
Rough, pictish hordes scrabbling
Like bodied clouds
Drain away into our sealed ducts
From bare hills.

Though proofed against most of their
Uncivil, natural subversions,
We, too, invent,
Within bedded walls, our own
Distanced localities,

The unmapped settlements only we
Can find a way to, where a train
Stops by a sign
At the rail-head, near the new
Workers' co-op.

Helevyn the letters say. Cyrillic
Or Gaelic? The paint glistens.
Stacked with soft peat,
A line of yellow trucks shunts out
To the power-station;

While, on afforested slopes,
Chain-saws bite into spruce and fir.
The pine huts
Everyone lives in fresh keenly
Of green juniper;

Their strenuous inhabitants smile
In a chill light, then go on working.
They know all the
Objections to this bracken frontier,
Lawless, chastening;

And if their loves are seldom easy
Their only authorities are those
Black, cairnless summits,
And these their energetic combines
Are subduing.

Ballywaire

My loathsome uncle chews his rasher,
My aunt is mother, pouring tea,
And this is where I live: a town
On the wrong side of the border.

A town the mountain simplifies
To spires and roofs, a bridge that spans
The river – distance shines it – and joins
Packed rural terraces. They're workless,
Costive as the smell of groceries.

Through gunfire, night arrests and searches –
The crossroads loony smashed to bits –
I keep myself intact. My body purifies.
I'll never use it.

The air greys and lights come on
In curtained parlours, our clock ticks
By last year's calendar. The quiet.
An oleograph of Pity in each kitchen.
My heart is stone. I will not budge.

Newness

Cool to our bodies, the fresh linen pleats
And valances that met our eyes then.

He pressed my hand, my lover, my husband;
Held them both underwater in the wide bowl.

It was still night when I heard
The tramp of clogs to the mill.
Frost on the cobbles, I thought;
Hard wood is worn by the stone,
So is stone by the softness of feet.

Arthur

Everyone's got someone who gave them oranges,
Sovereigns or rubbed florins,
Who wore bottle-green blazers, smoked
A churchwarden pipe on St Swithin's day,
And mulled their ale by dousing red-hot pokers
In quart jars.
But you, you're different.
You pushed off before the millions wrapped their puttees on
And ran away to sea, the prairies, New York
Where they threw you in jail when you told someone
Your blond hair made you a German spy.
After the telegram demanding

[337]

Your birth certificate
No one on the Island knew anything about you
Until the Armistice brought a letter
From a wife they'd never heard of.
You'd left her with the baby.
She wanted money.
You were somewhere in South America
In the greatest freedom, the freedom
Of nothing-was-ever-heard-of-him-since.

So I see you sometimes
Paddling up the Orinoco or the River Plate
With rifle, trusty mongrel and native mistress,
Passing cities of abandoned stucco
Draped with lianas and anacondas,
Passing their derelict opera houses
Where Caruso used to warble
Among a million bottles of imported bubbly.
Or else I watch you among the packing-case republics,
Drinking rum at the seafront in Buenos Aires
And waiting for your luck to change;
The warm sticky nights, the news from Europe,
Then the war criminals settling like bats
In the greasy darkness.

Your sister thought she saw your face once
In a crowd scene –
She went to the cinema for a week, watching
For your pale moment. She thinks
You're still alive, sitting back
On the veranda of your hacienda,
My lost great uncle, the blond
Indestructible dare-devil
Who was always playing truant and jumping
Off the harbour wall.

What I want to know is
How you did it.
How you threw off an inherited caution
Or just never knew it.
I think your grave is lost
In the mush of a tropical continent.
You are a memory that blipped out.
And though they named you from the king
Who's supposed to wake and come back
Some day,
I know that if you turned up on my doorstep,
An old sea dog with a worn leather belt
And a face I'd seen somewhere before,
You'd get no welcome.
I'd want you away.

Personal Column

These messages are secret, the initials
Code them, puzzling most of us. 'LY
Where are you now? I love you still. MN.'
And then, next evening, 'MN are you still there?
Loving you. LY.' Until, 'Shall I write
To old address?' MN suggests, waiting.

Each teatime, the thin signals start again.
You can almost hear the cheeping
Of separated loves, obscure adulteries
That finished in pub carparks, though they want
To make it new, to meet again, furtively,
Like spies whose thoughts touch before their bodies can.

Love, in an empty warehouse, might be like this.
To think small print, so public, can be tender.
Who'd guess that in a city where the news
Is normal, so many men and women wait
For the paper-boy, their go-between, to bring them
Lonely but hopeful, to a bed somewhere?

Song for February

In a dull and metric month,
A season of dank cardboard,
There is a cheery trill
Of schmaltz and egg whisks
Behind the double-glazing
Of a million spongy lounges.
Light verse is now the norm

And academic fellows
File limericks by the score.
In a brute and sallow light
Like the cheeks of an average
Punk, dead-headed roses waste
Over the pocked snow . . .
A fucked-up future snubs

The deadlands of the mullahs
Where young men dream of laws
As simple as the gallows.
And tonto in the dreck
Below the thermocline
An appetite for sex
Exhausts its fantasies.

Bored and parched, a torpid hack
Ghosts a tenth-rate life
Of President Sunsetsuma,
While Apollo pulls a string
Of ersatz novels from his lips.
The angel chimes go *ting-a-ling*
And the sugar hostess weeps

One year in four, but more and more.

Still Century

The hard captains of industry
Held the province in a firm control.

Judges, your pious tyranny
Is baked bone-dry in the old

Bricks of a hundred linen mills,
The shadows of black tabernacles.

A crowd moves along the Shankill,
And lamps shine in the dull

Streets where a fierce religion
Prays to the names of power:

Ewart and Bryson, Craig and Carson.
On every wall, texts or a thick char.

Stacked in the corners of factory-yards,
The wicker carboys of green acid

Hold out their bitter promise of whiteness
To the bleachgreens above the city.

The orange smoke at sunset, the gruff
Accents of a thousand foremen, speak

To the chosen, saying they are the stuff
That visions, cutlery and Belleek

China are laid on. They are tied
To the shade of a bearded god,

Their dream of happiness is his smile
And his skilful way with the hardest rod.

Anastasia McLaughlin

Her father is sick. He dozes most afternoons.
The nurse makes tea then and scans *The Newsletter*.
She has little to say to his grey daughter
Whose name began a strangeness the years took over.
His trade was flax and yarns, he brought her name
With an ikon and *matrioshka* – gifts for his wife
Who died the year that Carson's statue was unveiled.

McLaughlin is dreaming of a sermon he once heard
From a righteous preacher in a wooden pulpit
Who frowned upon a sinful brotherhood and shouted
The Word of deserts and rainy places where the Just
Are stretched to do the work a hard God sent them for.
His text was taken from the land of Uz
Where men are upright and their farms are walled.

'Though we may make sand to melt in a furnace
And make a mirror of it, we are as shadows
Thrown by a weaver's shuttle: and though we hide

ourselves

In desolate cities and in empty houses,
His anger will seek us out till we shall hear
The accent of the destroyer, the sly champing
Of moths busy with the linen in our chests.'

He wakes to a dull afternoon like any other –
The musty dampness of his study, the window panes
That flaw his view of the lawn and settled trees.
The logs in the grate have turned to a soft ash.
The dour gardener who cut them is smoking
In the warm greenhouse, wondering did his nephew
Break in the week before and thieve McLaughlin's silver?

Constables came to the Mill House with alsatians,
And the wet spring was filled with uniforms and statements.
When they found nothing, they suspected everyone.
Even the plain woman who served them tea.
'Father, I am the lost daughter whose name you stole.
Your visions slide across these walls: dry lavender,
Old memories of all that wronged us. I am unkind.'

[344]

He sees his son below the bruised Atlantic,
And on a summer's morning in Great Victoria Street
He talks with Thomas Ferguson outside the Iceworks.
He sees the north stretched out upon the mountains,
Its dream of fair weather rubbing a bloom on rinsed slates;
He watches the mills prosper and grow derelict,
As he starts his journey to the Finland Station.

Where Art is a Midwife

In the third decade of March,
A Tuesday in the town of Z—

The censors are on day-release.
They must learn about literature.

There are things called ironies,
Also symbols, which carry meaning.

The types of ambiguity
Are as numerous as the enemies

Of the state. Formal and bourgeois,
Sonnets sing of the old order,

Its lost gardens where white ladies
Are served wine in the subtle shade.

[345]

This poem about a bear
Is not a poem about a bear.

It might be termed a satire
On a loyal friend. Do I need

To spell it out? Is it possible
That none of you can understand?

The Other Voice

Anglican firelight.
Jugged hare in a stone house.
The gowned schoolmaster

Has a saintly politeness.
'It is possible to wonder,'
I hear him say.

The wind soughs in the demesne.
Exiles light a candle
To the gods of place.

In the winter darkness
Of this mild village
There is the mossy fragrance

Of damp branches under leaves,
The sour yeast of fungus.
At the lighted doorway

I forget to shake hands.
'We must meet again,' he calls,
And I pretend to pretend.

*

I make that crossing again
And catch the salt freshness
Of early light on Queen's Island.

I lay claim to those marshes,
The Lagan, the shipyards,
The Ormeau Road in winter.

That back room off Donegall Pass,
Remember, where the cell met?
That cupboard of books, tracts and poems?

Plekhanov flares like a firework,
Trotsky crosses Siberia
Turning the pages of Homer,

Raskolnikov wears a long coat
And the end justifies the means.
'Soon the rosewood *meubles*

Will shake in the drawing-rooms
On the Malone Road.
After the long marches

There will be shares for us all
In the means of production.
Songs of a new society

Will grow like flowers
From the barrel of a gun.
It's easy. It's easy.

Love is all you need.'
The record sticks and the party
Spins on forever.

*

We wished it could happen.
Less often now, I wish it still.
For it seems like a barren

Simplicity with no ghosts.
And those dreams of gardens
Called me from the way, saying:

'Here are the small mercies,
A glass of wine, the pungent shade,
And a cagey friendship.

Grace is a volume of Horace,
Bishops and pigeons
Cooing in a woggles shire.

Life, my dear, is a fixed order
And your verse should flow
With a touching sweetness.

Better a civil twilight
Than the level emptiness
Of pulp culture.'

*

In the visions of the night
When deep sleep falls on men,
The flickering pictures

Pass before our eyes.
The fear of necessity
In an absolute narrative.

History is happening:
Tanks and caterpillars,
A moth lying in the dust.

'Once, in Odessa, I watched
The governor cursing.
His back was turned in the hot square.

A regiment with bark sandals,
A sprig of green in their caps.
Their tragedy scorched my mind.

Those bark sandals, those green sprigs!
But the process of history
Must scorn an emotion.

I am history now.
I carry time in my mind.
As sharp as an axe.'

*

The actors shake their fists.
I hear the same opinions
In a muddy light.

I see a regiment of clones
Waving their arms and shouting:
A glossy brutalism dances

To a parody of song.
Identikit opinions
In the camps of the punks.

The theatre is in the streets,
The streets are in the theatre,
The poet is torn to pieces.

*

What does a poem serve?
Only the pure circle of itself.
Now, between two coasts,

The servants of the state
Doze to the drum of engines.
Hammered stars, a dark dream,

The hard night in a dead bowl.
Where a free light wakes
To its spacious language

Choice is still possible.
I dream of a subtle voice,
Stare in a mirror and pray

To a shadow wandering
Beyond the cold shores
And tides of the Baltic.

*

In Buddhist Moscow,
In lamp-eyed St Petersburg,
Mandelstam is walking

Through the terrible night.
His lips are moving
In a lyric ripple.

The syllables chirp
Like a dolphin, lost
In the grey depths of the state.

'As I walk through the dark
I will tell you this:
That morning, in the buttery

Of the Kremlin, I left
Because I could never stay
In the same room as Trotsky.

Do you understand me?
Those ideals will fit you
Like a feral uniform.

Hear how the wolves howl,
Functions of nature
On the frozen plains.

All the dry glitters
In your cento of memories
Will never catch

The living truth on the wing.
The bird has flown its nest
And the snow weighs

On the gothic branches,
Lavish and cruel, like power.
What cadences, what rich voices

Have you hardened against?
What images have you broken?
In the great dome of art

(It was this we longed for
In our Petropolis)
I am free of history.

Beyond dust and rhetoric,
In the meadows of the spirit
I kiss the Word.'

Desertmartin

At noon, in the dead centre of a faith,
Between Draperstown and Magherafelt,
This bitter village shows the flag
In a baked absolute September light.
Here the Word has withered to a few
Parched certainties, and the charred stubble
Tightens like a black belt, a crop of Bibles.

Because this is the territory of the Law
I drive across it with a powerless knowledge –
The owl of Minerva in a hired car.
A Jock squaddy glances down the street
And grins, happy and expendable,
Like a brass cartridge. He is a useful thing,
Almost at home, and yet not quite, not quite.

It's a limed nest, this place. I see a plain
Presbyterian grace sour, then harden,
As a free strenuous spirit changes
To a servile defiance that whines and shrieks
For the bondage of the letter: it shouts
For the Big Man to lead his wee people
To a clean white prison, their scorched tomorrow.

Masculine Islam, the rule of the Just,
Egyptian sand dunes and geometry,
A theology of rifle-butts and executions:
These are the places where the spirit dies.
And now, in Desertmartin's sandy light,
I see a culture of twigs and bird-shit
Waving a gaudy flag it loves and curses.

Descendancy

All those family histories
are like sucking a polo mint –
you're pulled right through
a tight wee sphincter
that loses you.
e.g. I've a second cousin
drives a prowl car
in downtown Vancouver,
and another's the local rozzer
in a place called Buxton.

Could be that a third one
– say an ex-B Special –
has pulled up at a roadblock
a shade far from Garrison?

The Book of Juniper

In the original liturgy
on a bare island

a voice seeks an answer
in the sea wind

'The tides parted and I crossed
barefoot to Inishkeel.

Where was the lost crozier
among the scorched bracken?

And where was that freshet
of sweet water?

Goose-grass and broken walls
were all my sanctuary,

I mistook a drowsed hour
for the spirit's joy;

on a thymy headland
I entered

the strict soul
of a dry cricket.

Heat haze and wild flowers,
a warm chirring all

that civil afternoon,
till its classic song

failed me and I sighed
for a different love

in grey weather.'

*

'Place the yeasty word
between my lips,

give me comfort
in a sheepfold,

shelter me
in a mild grove.'

*

'There is no word
and no comfort.

Only a lichened stone
is given you,

and juniper,
green juniper.'

*

Tougher than the wind
it keeps a low profile
on rough ground.
Rugged, fecund,
with resined spines,
the gymnosperm
hugs the hillside
and wills its own survival.
The subtle arts are still to happen
and in the eye of a needle
a singing voice
tells a miniature epic
of the boreal forest:
not a silk tapestry
of fierce folk
warring on the tundra
or making exquisite love
on a starry counterpane,
but an in-the-beginning
was a wintry light
and *juniperus*.

*

On the brown hills
above a Roman spa
in Austro-Hungaria
the savin hides
its berries of blue wax
in a thorny crown,
while in the rapt
shaded casino
a small black ball
skips and ricochets
like a sniper's bullet.

Jug-ears and jowls,
walrus moustaches, frowns –
those gravid urns
on clotted mahogany.
What mineral water can soothe
a tetchy liver or a glum colon?

The wheel flicks,
the hard pea itches;
in the gummed hotel
fingers dibble and thrust
like sappers pushing
through primed earth.

Later, the dry scrape
of an empty tumbler
locked on a ouija board
will spell out a dead yes
like chalk on a billiard cue.

The wind riffles the savin;
the humid band begins to play.

*

A clear and tearful fluid,
the bittersweet genièvre
is held to a wet window
above a college garden.

On the lazy shores
of a tideless sea,
the Phoenician juniper
burns a fragrant incense
in a sandy nest.

And in a Zen garden
all the miniature trees
have the perfect despair
of bound feet.

Exiled in Voronezh
the leavening priest of the Word
receives the Host on his tongue –
frost, stars, a dark berry,
and the sun is buried at midnight.

*

On a bruised coast
I crush a blue bead
between my fingers,
tracing the scent, somewhere,
of that warm mnemonic haybox,
burnished fields, a linen picnic
and a summer dawn
where mushrooms raise their domed gills.
They are white in the dew
and this nordic grape
whets an eager moment
of bodies meeting in a fishy fume.
Its meek astringency is distilled
into perfume and medicines,
it matches venison
as the sour gooseberry
cuts the oily mackerel.
Spicy, glaucous,
its branches fan out
like the wind's shadow
on long grass,

then melt back
and go to ground
where swart choughs
open their red beaks,
stinging the air
with stony voices.

*

Though it might be a simple
decoration
or a chill fragrance
in a snug souterrain,
I must grasp again
how its green
springy resistance
ducks its head down and skirts
the warped polities of other trees
bent in the Atlantic wind.
For no one knows
if nature allowed it
to grow tall
what proud grace
the juniper tree might show
that flared, once, like fire
along the hills.

*

On this coast
it is the only
tree of freedom
to be found,
and I imagine
that a swelling army is marching
from Memory Harbour and Killala
carrying branches
of green juniper.

Consider
the gothic zigzags
and brisk formations
that square to meet
the green tide rising
through Mayo and Antrim,

now dream
of that sweet
equal republic
where the juniper
talks to the oak,
the thistle,
the bandaged elm,
and the jolly jolly chestnut.

Politik

The headmaster of a national school
chalks *Ginkel* on the blackboard
as a flag snicks a big *NO*
over the mudflats and barracks;
the city is like a locked yard
that's caked with grey pigeon-cack;
the Chief stalks, stalks, like the Kaiser
and crowds bristle at the docks.
Krekk! kkrek! the stubborn particles
trek through my carbon-dater,
each chipping past like a spiked curse
stamped with these numbers: 1–9–1–2.

I'd be dead chuffed if I could catch
the dialects of those sea-loughs,
but I'm scared of all that's hard
and completely subjective:
those quartzy voices in the playground
of a school called Rosetta Primary
whose basalt and sandstone have gone
like Napoleon into Egypt.

Off the Back of a Lorry

A zippo lighter
and a quilted jacket,
two rednecks troughing
in a gleamy diner,
the flinty chipmarks
on a white enamel pail,
Paisley putting pen to paper
in Crumlin jail,
a jumbo double
fried peanut butter
sandwich Elvis scoffed
during the last
diapered days –
they're more than tacky,
these pured fictions,
and like the small ads
in a country paper
they build a gritty
sort of prod baroque
I must return to
like my own boke.

A Rum Cove, a Stout Cove

On the Barrack Islands far out
in the South Atlantic
the great-great-grandson (Sol Grout)
of Nelson's last bosun
is packing crawfish into a thick
barnacled keepbox marked *Briton
Kanning Factors Illimitated*.
It's his swart locks and cochin cheeks
that glim in the top left-hand corner
of 'Bold Bessie', the prime banner
that longs to LOL 301.
Like Gib, like the god called M'Lud,
and those tars behind locked doors
whistling *Britannia Rules*
in their slow skrimshandering
with worn and corded tools,
he's firm, Sol Grout, to the core,
the genius of these used islands
where no maritime elegists sing
of Resolution or Independence
with their harbourmaster's stores,
clagged mountains of ashy shale
and a small bird that no one has named –
a flightless timorous landrail
whose cry is rusted, hard, like chains.

A Written Answer

This poem by Rupert Brookeborough
is all about fishing and the stout B-men
(they live for always in our hearts,
their only crime was being loyal),
there is a lough in it and stacks of rivers,
also a brave wee hymn to the sten-gun.
The poet describes Gough of the Curragh
and by his use of many metric arts
he designs a fictionary universe
which has its own laws and isn't quite
the same as this place that we call real.
His use of metonymy is pretty desperate
and the green symbolism's a contradiction,
but I like his image of the elm and chestnut,
for to me this author is a fly man
and the critics yonder say his work is alright.

Manichean Geography I

Consider a coral or guano atoll
Where a breezy Union Jack
Flaps above the police station.

There is a rusting mission hut
Built out of flattened tin cans
(Bully beef, beans and tomato pilchards)

Where the Reverend Bungo Buller
And his prophet, Joe Gimlet,
Preach the gospel of cargoes.

They worship a white god
Of dentures and worn toothbrushes
Who will come to earth, Hallelulia,

In a reconditioned Flying Fortress
Humping bales of fresh calico
And a crate of Black and Deckers.

Seeding like brisk parachutes,
The ancestral spirits will fall
From the pod of an airship,

And the chosen people will serve
Themselves with orange jube-jubes
In a brand-new discount warehouse.

Of Difference Does it Make

During the 51-year existence of the Northern Ireland Parliament
only one Bill sponsored by a non-Unionist member was ever
passed.

Among the plovers and the stonechats
protected by the Wild Birds Act
of nineteen-hundred-and-thirty-one,
there is a rare stint called the notawhit
that has a schisty flight-call, like the chough's.
Notawhit, notawhit, notawhit
– it raps out a sharp code-sign
like a mild and patient prisoner
pecking through granite with a teaspoon.

And Where Do You Stand on the National Question?

'Told him the shortest way to Tara was via Holyhead.'
(Stephen Dedalus)

Apple-blossom, a great spread of it
above our heads.
This blue morning a new visitor
is laidback on a deckchair;
he's civil and clever,
a flinty mandarin
being entertained, like an oxymoron,
in this walled garden.
Ecco two glasses of young wine
. . . *et on mange des asperges.*

I imagine him
as the state's intelligence,
a lean man in a linen suit
who has come to question me
for picking up a pen
and taking myself a shade seriously.
'Paisley's plain tongue, his cult
of Bunyan and blood
in blind dumps like Doagh and Boardmills –
that's the enemy.'
I've an answer ready in the sun
but my eye tines the grass
for a tiny mound of soil:
the mole works underground,
a blind glove
that gropes the earth and cannot love.
'Your Lagan Jacobins, they've gone
with *The Northern Star*. I've heard
Hewitt and Heaney trace us back
to the Antrim weavers –
I can't come from *that*.'
'Why not, though? Isn't there
this local stir in us all? –
flick of the thumb, a word's relish,
the clitoral tick of an accent,
wee lick of spit or lovejuice?
I'd call that a brave kindness.'
Then a journey blows back at me –
rust-orange and green,
the Enterprise scudding north
past the brown burn of whin and bracken
till it halts and waits for clearance

under the gourly vigilance
of a corrie in bandit country –
'That's where the god, Autochthon,
is crossed by the hangman's rope.'
He counters with a short fiction
called *Molyneaux's Last Hope*.
'These islands are stepping-stones
to a metropolitan home,
an archipelago that's strung
between America and Europe.'
'So you're a band of Orange dandies?
Oscar in Père-Lachaise with a sash on?'
'Well, not exactly . . . that's unfair –
like my saying it's a green mess you're after.'
'I want a form that's classic and secular,
the risen *République*,
a new song for a new constitution –
wouldn't you rather have that
than stay loose, baggy and British?
You don't *have* to fall back
on Burke and the Cruiser,
on a batty style
and slack o'whoozy emotion.'
We hit a pause like a ramp,
shrug and mark time
before we guess the design
of life after Prior:
the last civil servant
is dropping over from Whitehall.
Call him Sir Peregrine Falkland;
he's a bit thick – not a high-flyer –
but he'll do the trick.

MEDBH McGUCKIAN   1950–

Smoke

They set the whins on fire along the road.
I wonder what controls it, can the wind hold
That snake of orange motion to the hills,
Away from the houses?

They seem so sure what they can do.
I am unable even
To contain myself, I run
Till the fawn smoke settles on the earth.

Tobacco Hole

The rubbing boats mark the twin churches,
The priest's ravine, the rector's gentle bushes,
Donal's lamp in line with Isaac's-on-the-Hill,
Green Harbour dodging Kibby's Mill.

The women bait the thorns with half-blood knots.
Their carts assemble in the driftweed moon
Near Lady Annesley's fish-traps, where the heron
Is shot in the low tide.

The lifter herds are summering on poverty mountain.
The black bog from the meadow of the deer
To the wood of wild garlic, the vanishing lake,
Is white as the bride's show.

There's no skin from the wooden plough.
On the washed-up ladder farms; the foals' tails
Shine with the pulp of the whin, like the coastguard's
                                        windlight
In the tarted-up houses, widows' row.

June

Now we are like a snail,
Low in blood, in lowest gear,
Trailing silver, shelled in music
Through this flowering frontispiece.

Listen, we are engraved in snow,
The windscreen dissolves in a slow
Embroidered thaw, we are Kay
And Gerda, under a white tent.

Gateposts

A man will keep a horse for prestige,
But a woman ripens best underground.
He settles where the wind
Brings his whirling hat to rest,
And the wind decides which door is to be used.

[374]

Under the hip-roofed thatch,
The bed-wing is warmed by the chimney breast;
On either side the keeping-holes
For his belongings, hers.

He says it's unlucky to widen the house,
And leaves the gateposts holding up the fairies.
He lays his lazy-beds and burns the river,
He builds turf-castles,
And sprigs the corn with apple-mint.

She spreads heather on the floor
And sifts the oatmeal ark for thin-bread farls:
All through the blue month
She tosses stones in basins to the sun,
And watches for the trout in the holy well.

The Cure

What is more beautiful than potatoes in bloom?
A red-head swinging poteen from her breasts,
A smuggler from the cradle, with no character to lose,
She gives no dry bargains, she's the dough in the still.

Grain sprouts under the bed, steeps in the false gable,
To keep Red Willy's tongue as rough as corduroy.
It would make a rabbit spit at a dog
To see it swallowed by hat-makers, french-polishers.

[375]

Once a man gets land, he loses his thirst.
They should have been canonized who sprayed
Water on the worm, vapour from the kettle's nipple:
In the diocese of Derry it's a reserved sin.

Tulips

Touching the tulips was a shyness
I had had for a long time – such
Defensive mechanisms to frustrate the rain
That shakes into the sherry-glass
Of the daffodil, though scarcely
Love's young dream; such present-mindedness
To double-lock in tiers as whistle-tight,
Or catch up on sleep with cantilevered
Palms cupping elbows. It's their independence
Tempts them to this grocery of soul.

Except, like all governesses, easily
Carried away, in sunny
Absences of mirrors they exalt themselves
To ballets of revenge, a kind
Of twinness, an olympic way of earning,
And are sacrificed to plot, their faces
Lifted many times to the artistry of light –
Its lovelessness a deeper sort
Of illness than the womanliness
Of tulips with their bee-dark hearts.

Mr McGregor's Garden

Some women save their sanity with needles.
I complicate my life with studies
Of my favourite rabbit's head, his vulgar volatility,
Or a little ladylike sketching
Of my resident toad in his flannel box;
Or search for handsome fungi for my tropical
Herbarium, growing dry-rot in the garden,
And wishing that the climate were kinder,
Turning over the spiky purple heads among the moss
With my cheese-knife to view the slimy veil.

Unlike the cupboard-love of sleepers in the siding,
My hedgehog's sleep is under his control
And not the weather's; he can rouse himself
At half-an-hour's notice in the frost, or leave at will
On a wet day in August, by the hearth.
He goes by breathing slowly, after a large meal,
A lively evening, very cross if interrupted,
And returns with a hundred respirations
To the minute, weak and nervous when he wakens,
Busy with his laundry.

On sleepless nights while learning
Shakespeare off by heart,
I feel that Bunny's at my bedside
In a white cotton nightcap,
Tickling me with his whiskers.

The Sofa

Do not be angry if I tell you
Your letter stayed unopened on my table
For several days. If you were friend enough
To believe me, I was about to start writing
At any moment; my mind was savagely made up,
Like a serious sofa moved
Under a north window. My heart, alas,

Is not the calmest of places.
Still it is not my heart that needs replacing:
And my books seem real enough to me,
My disasters, my surrenders, all my loss . . .
Since I was child enough to forget
That you loathe poetry, you ask for some –
About nature, greenery, insects, and of course,

The sun – surely that would be to open
An already open window? Celebrating
The impudence of flowers? If I could
Interest you instead in his large, gentle stares,
How his soft shirt is the inside of pleasure
To me, why I must wear white for him,
Imagine he no longer trembles

When I approach, no longer buys me
Flowers for my name day . . . But I spread
On like a house, I begin to scatter
To a tiny to-and-fro at odds
With the wear on my threshold. Somewhere
A curtain rising wonders where I am,
My books sleep, pretending to forget me.

Slips

The studied poverty of a moon roof,
The earthenware of dairies cooled by apple trees,
The apple tree that makes the whitest wash . . .

But I forget names, remembering them wrongly
Where they touch upon another name,
A town in France like a woman's Christian name.

My childhood is preserved as a nation's history,
My favourite fairy tales the shells
Leased by the hermit crab.

I see my grandmother's death as a piece of ice,
My mother's slimness restored to her,
My own key slotted in your door –

Tricks you might guess from this unfastened button,
A pen mislaid, a word misread,
My hair coming down in the middle of a conversation.

To my Grandmother

I would revive you with a swallow's nest:
For as long a time as I could hold my breath
I would feel your pulse like tangled weeds
Separate into pearls. The heart should rule
The summer, ringing like a sickle over
The need to make life hard. I would
Sedate your eyes with rippleseed, those
Hollow points that close as if
Your eyelids had been severed to
Deny you sleep, imagine you a dawn.
I would push a chrysanthemum stone
Into your sleeve without your noticing
Its reaching far, its going, its returning.
When the end of summer comes, it is
A season by itself; when your tongue
Curls back like a sparrow's buried head,
I would fill your mouth with rice and mussels.

The Seed-Picture

This is my portrait of Joanna – since the split
The children come to me like a dumb-waiter,
And I wonder where to put them, beautiful seeds
With no immediate application . . . the clairvoyance
Of seed-work has opened up
New spectrums of activity, beyond a second home.

[380]

The seeds dictate their own vocabulary,
Their dusty colours capture
More than we can plan,
The mould on walls, or jumbled garages,
Dead flower heads where insects shack . . .
I only guide them not by guesswork
In their necessary numbers,
And attach them by the spine to a perfect bedding,
Woody orange pips, and tear-drop apple,
The banana of the caraway, wrinkled pepper-corns,
The pocked peach, or waterlily honesty,
The seamed cherry stone so hard to break.

Was it such self-indulgence to enclose her
In the border of a grandmother's sampler,
Bonding all the seeds in one continuous skin,
The sky resolved to a cloud the length of a man?
To use tan linseed for the trees, spiky
Sunflower for leaves, bright lentils
For the window, patna stars
For the floral blouse? Her hair
Is made of hook-shaped marigold, gold
Of pleasure for her lips, like raspberry grain.
The eyelids oatmeal, the irises
Of Dutch blue maw, black rape
For the pupils, millet
For the vicious beige circles underneath.
The single pearl barley
That sleeps around her dullness
Till it catches light, makes women
Feel their age, and sigh for liberation.

Champagne

The soulless matchmaking of lunar moths,
Uncanny, delicate or helpful, dove-coloured
Bosoms in the night: their fictions hurt us
Gently, like the nudity of rose-beige tea-gowns . . .

The mayflies' opera is their only moon, only
Those that fall on water reproduce, content
With scattering in fog or storm, such ivory
As elephants hold lofty, like champagne.

The Flower Master

Like foxgloves in the school of the grass moon
We come to terms with shade, with the principle
Of enfolding space. Our scissors in brocade,
We learn the coolness of straight edges, how
To gently stroke the necks of daffodils
And make them throw their heads back to the sun.

We slip the thready stems of violets, delay
The loveliness of the hibiscus dawn with quiet ovals,
Spirals of feverfew like water splashing,
The papery legacies of bluebells. We do
Sea-fans with sea-lavender, moon-arrangements
Roughly for the festival of moon-viewing.

This black container calls for sloes, sweet
Sultan, dainty nipplewort, in honour
Of a special guest, who summoned to the
Tea ceremony, must stoop to our low doorway,
Our fontanelle, the trout's dimpled feet.

The Standing

This is my day-by-day book, my open-air
Oratory, of that tenacious month, so little
News, uncertain weather, I began to see
Light through the curtains of my sick-room.

My godmother, an understanding kinswoman,
Had taught me, her namesake, almost natural
Daughter, cushion-making – Irish stitch
On cloth-of-silver – how to restring

Loose drop-shaded pearls, such static
Occupations . . . I remembered keeping silkworms
As a little girl, my everlasting embroidery;
How my mother lay with me, her surreptitious

Kindness . . . I remember her face of that day,
Its sleep enforced like malefactors
Lodged in the lowest storey of the keep,

The Pagan Tower: her feet just clear
Of a recumbent lamb, her dress unwrinkled
Like the Rhône passing through Geneva.

The Moon Pond

I thought this morning of my yellowed Juliette cap,
Its head-dress of artificial pearls that I wore once,
And never wore again . . . It is not the same
With this bright moon pond where, they say,
If you come once you'll likely come again,
Fed slowly by the natural canal, where swims the otter
You were dreaming had made you pregnant.

As with an egg I close my mouth, with an egg
I open it again, my May Day rising, after
My warrior's sleep, and crossing the fat churchyard
Left by a green Christmas, the souls of the dead
As thick as bees in an uncut meadow round me.
I leave a bowl of spring water womanly on the table
For your wild and nameless sprays before they withered.

I leave a stack of salt fallen from a thimble,
A measure of milk with a cock's step of butter,
Coming in hills and going in mountains:
For this milk-fevered lady is the round-eyed child
Listening with bated breath to the singalong
Of birds that, waking in the heart of rain,
Would just as boldly start to mate again.

The Aphrodisiac

She gave it out as if it were
A marriage or a birth, some other
Interesting family event, that she
Had finished sleeping with him, that
Her lover was her friend. It was his heart
She wanted, the bright key to his study,
Not the menacings of love. So he is
Banished to his estates, to live
Like a man in a glasshouse; she has taken to
A little cap of fine white lace
In the mornings, feeds her baby
In a garden you could visit blindfold
For its scent alone:
                But though a ray of grace
Has fallen, all her books seem as frumpish
As the last year's gambling game, when she
Would dress in pink taffeta, and drive
A blue phaeton, or in blue, and drive
A pink one, with her black hair supported
By a diamond comb, floating about
Without panniers. How his most
Caressing look, his husky whisper suffocates her,
This almost perfect power of knowing
More than a kept woman. The between-maid
Tells me this is not the only secret staircase.
Rumour has it she's taken to rouge again.

Power-Cut

The moon is salmon as a postage-stamp
Over the tonsured trees, a rise-and-fall lamp
In a cracked ice ceiling. The cruelty
Of road conditions flushes summer near,
As the storm seal hangs along the pier.

My dishes on the draining-board
Lie at an even keel, the baby lowered
Into his lobster-pot pen; my sponge
Disintegrates in water like a bird's nest,
A permanent wave gone west.

These plotted holes of days my keep-net shades,
Soluble as refuse in canals; the old flame
Of the candle sweats in the night, its hump
A dowager's with bones running thin:
The door-butler lets the strangers in.

The Flitting

'You wouldn't believe all this house has cost me –
In body-language terms, it has turned me upside down.'
I've been carried from one structure to the other
On a chair of human arms, and liked the feel
Of being weightless, that fraternity of clothes . . .
Now my own life hits me in the throat, the bumps
And cuts of the walls as telling
As the poreholes in strawberries, tomato seeds.
I cover them for safety with these Dutch girls
Making lace, or leaning their almond faces
On their fingers with a mandolin, a dreamy
Chapelled ease abreast this other turquoise-turbanned,
Glancing over her shoulder with parted mouth.

She seems a garden escape in her unconscious
Solidarity with darkness, clove-scented
As an orchid taking fifteen years to bloom,
And turning clockwise as the honeysuckle.
Who knows what importance
She attaches to the hours?
Her narrative secretes its own values, as mine might
If I painted the half of me that welcomes death
In a faggotted dress, in a peacock chair,
No falser biography than our casual talk
Of losing a virginity, or taking a life, and
No less poignant if dying
Should consist in more than waiting.

I postpone my immortality for my children,
Little rock-roses, cushioned
In long-flowering sea-thrift and metrics,
Lacking elemental memories:
I am well-earthed here as the digital clock,
Its numbers flicking into place like overgrown farthings
On a bank where once a train
Ploughed like an emperor living out a myth
Through the cambered flesh of clover and wild carrot.

On not being your Lover

Your eyes were ever brown, the colour
Of time's submissiveness. Love nerves
Or a heart, beat in their world of
Privilege, I had not yet kissed you
On the mouth.

But I would not say, in my un-freedom
I had weakly drifted there, like the
Bone-deep blue that visits and decants
The eyes of our children:

How warm and well-spaced their dreams
You can tell from the sleep-late mornings
Taken out of my face! Each lighted
Window shows me cardiganed, more desolate
Than the garden, and more hallowed
Than the hinge of the brass-studded
Door that we close, and no one opens,
That we open and no one closes.

In a far-flung, too young part,
I remembered all your slender but
Persistent volume said, friendly, complex
As the needs of your new and childfree girl.

Aviary

Well may you question the degree of falsehood
In my round-the-house men's clothes, when I seem
Cloaked for a journey, after just relearning to walk,
Or turning a swarthy aspect like a cache-
Enfant against all men. Some patterns have
A very long repeat, and this includes a rose
Which has much in common with the rose
In your drawing, where you somehow put the garden
To rights. You call me aspen, tree of the woman's
Tongue, but if my longer and longer sentences
Prove me wholly female, I'd be persimmon,
And good kindling, to us both.
Remember
The overexcitement of mirrors, with their archways
Lending depth, until my compact selvedge
Frisks into a picot-edged valance, some
Swiss-fronted little shop? All this is as it
Should be, the disguise until those clear red
Bands of summerwood accommodate next
Winter's tardy ghost, your difficult daughter.

I can hear already in my chambered pith
The hammers of pianos, their fastigiate notes
Arranging a fine sight-screen for my nectary,
My trustful mop. And if you feel uncertain
Whether pendent foliage mitigates the damage
Done by snow, yet any wild bird would envy you
This aviary, whenever you free all the birds in me.

The Hard Summer

Then I was one long curve, from
The top of my head to my toes,
And an unseen arm kept me from
Falling over. My locked line
Was a kind of sweep, like the letter
S, diffusing as it pulled away
The light that came from below.
Your fingers found how breast
And arm change when they press
Together, how the bent leg
Hides even from the married
The H behind the knee. Though
Certain bones lie always
Next to the skin, an elbow
Forcing the back to crease
Might just be playing 'The Hard
Summer' for us, like a gift
That passes from father to daughter.

All that is month-named is
The T-shape of your face in the
Spring shadows, folds in your palm
That fall aside like breasts,
Creating the letter M.

Venus and the Rain

White on white, I can never be viewed
Against a heavy sky – my gibbous voice
Passes from leaf to leaf, retelling the story
Of its own provocative fractures, till
Their facing coasts might almost fill each other
And they ask me in reply if I've
Decided to stop trying to make diamonds.

On one occasion, I rang like a bell
For a whole month, promising their torn edges
The birth of a new ocean (as all of us
Who have hollow bodies tend to do at times):
What clues to distance could they have,
So self-excited by my sagging sea,
Widened ten times faster than it really did?

Whatever rivers sawed their present lairs
Through my lightest, still-warm rocks,
I told them they were only giving up
A sun for sun, that cruising moonships find
Those icy domes relaxing, when they take her
Rind to pieces, and a waterfall
Unstitching itself down the front stairs.

Felicia's Café

Darkness falls short by an hour
Of this summer's inhibitions:
Only the cold carpet
That owns a kind of flower,
Feeds any farm or ocean
Around the bedroom's heart.

Each day of brown perfection
May be colour enough for bees:
The part of my eye
That is not golden, sees.

Biographical Notes on Contributors

PATRICK KAVANAGH

Born in County Monaghan in 1904. His *Collected Poems* were first published in 1964 by Macgibbon and Kee.

LOUIS MACNEICE

Born in Belfast in 1907. His *Collected Poems* were published in 1966 by Faber and Faber.

THOMAS KINSELLA

Born in Dublin in 1928. His collections are *Poems* (1956), *Another September* (1958), *Moralities* (1960), *Downstream* (1962), *Wormwood* (1966), *Nightwalker* (1968), *One* (1974), *New Poems* (1975), *A Technical Supplement* (1976), *Song of the Night* (1978) and *The Messenger* (1978). His translation of the eighth-century Irish epic, *The Táin*, was published in 1969. *Poems 1956–1973* and *Peppercanister Poems 1972–1978* were published in 1979 by the Dolmen Press.

JOHN MONTAGUE

Born in Brooklyn, New York, in 1929. His collections are *Poisoned Lands* (1961), *A Chosen Light* (1967), *Tides* (1970), *The Rough Field* (1972), *A Slow Dance* (1975), *The Great Cloak* (1978) and *The Dead Kingdom* (1984). He has also published a book of short stories, *Death of a Chieftain* (1964) and edited *The Faber Book of Irish Verse* (1974). John Montague's *Selected Poems* were published in 1982 by the Dolmen Press.

MICHAEL LONGLEY

Born in Belfast in 1939. His collections are *No Continuing City* (1969), *An Exploded View* (1973), *Man Lying on a Wall* (1976) and *The Echo Gate* (1979). *Poems 1963–1983* was published in 1985 by the Salamander Press and Gallery Books.

SEAMUS HEANEY

Born in 1939 in County Derry. His collections are *Death of a Naturalist* (1966), *Door into the Dark* (1969), *Wintering Out* (1972), *North* (1975), *Field Work* (1979) and *Station Island* (1984). He has also published *Preoccupations: Selected Prose 1968–1978* (1980) and a version of the Middle Irish tale *Sweeney Astray* (1984). Seamus Heaney's *Selected Poems 1965–1975* appeared in 1980 from Faber and Faber.

DEREK MAHON

Born in Belfast in 1941. His collections are *Night-Crossing* (1968), *Lives* (1972), *The Snow Party* (1975) and *The Hunt by Night* (1982). Derek Mahon's *Poems 1962–1978* was published in 1979 by the Oxford University Press.

PAUL DURCAN

Born in Dublin in 1944. His books are *Endsville* (1967), *O Westport in the Light of Asia Minor* (1975), *Teresa's Bar* (1976), *Sam's Cross* (1978), *Jesus, Break His Fall* (1980), *Ark of the North* (1982) and *Jumping the Traintracks with Angela* (1984). *The Selected Paul Durcan*, edited by Edna Longley, was published in 1983 by the Blackstaff Press.

TOM PAULIN

Born in Leeds in 1949. His collections are *A State of Justice* (1977), *The Strange Museum* (1980) and *Liberty Tree* (1983). Tom Paulin has also published *Thomas Hardy: The Poetry of Perception* (1975) and a book of essays, *Ireland and the English Crisis* (1984).

MEDBH MCGUCKIAN

Born in 1950 in Belfast. Her books of poetry are *The Flower Master* (1982) and *Venus and the Rain* (1984).

Index of Titles

INDEX OF TITLES

INDEX OF TITLES

INDEX OF TITLES

INDEX OF TITLES

[399]

INDEX OF TITLES

[400]

INDEX OF TITLES

Index of First Lines

[403]

INDEX OF FIRST LINES

[407]

Acknowledgements

For permission to reprint copyright material the publishers gratefully acknowledge the following:

Blackstaff Press for 'Combe Florey', 'General Vallancey's Waltz', 'In Memory of Those Murdered in the Dublin Massacre, May 1974', 'Ireland 1972', 'Ireland 1977', 'The Kilfenora Teaboy', 'Letter to Ben, 1972', 'Making Love Outside Áras an Uachtaráin', 'Micheál Mac Liammóir', 'Nessa', 'November 1967', 'Sally', 'They Say the Butterfly is the Hardest Stroke' from *The Selected Paul Durcan* (1983), ed. Edna Longley; Faber & Faber Ltd and Farrar, Straus & Giroux Inc. for 'Follower', 'The Diviner', 'Personal Helicon' from *Death of a Naturalist* by Seamus Heaney; Faber & Faber Ltd and Farrar, Straus & Giroux Inc. for 'Bogland', 'The Forge', 'The Given Note', 'Night Drive', 'The Peninsula', 'The Plantation', 'Requiem for the Croppies', 'Thatcher' from *Door into the Dark* by Seamus Heaney; Faber & Faber Ltd and Farrar, Straus & Giroux Inc. for 'The Other Side', 'Summer Home', 'The Tollund Man', from *Wintering Out* by Seamus Heaney; Faber & Faber Ltd and Farrar, Straus & Giroux Inc. for 'Mossbawn: Two Poems in Dedication' from *North* by Seamus Heaney; Faber & Faber Ltd and Farrar, Straus & Giroux Inc. for 'A Dream of Jealousy', 'A Drink of Water', 'Field Work', 'The Harvest Bow', 'In Memoriam Francis Ledwidge', 'The Otter', 'A Postcard from North Antrim', 'The Skunk' from *Field Work* by Seamus Heaney; Faber & Faber Ltd and Farrar, Straus & Giroux Inc. for 'The Birthplace', 'Changes', 'A Hazel Stick for Catherine Ann', 'Sloe Gin', an excerpt from 'Station

ACKNOWLEDGEMENTS

Island', 'Widgeon' from *Station Island* by Seamus Heaney;
Mrs Katharine Kavanagh and Martín Brian & O'Keefe Ltd
for 'Advent', 'Art McCooey', 'Bluebells for Love', 'A
Christmas Childhood', 'Come Dance with Kitty Stobling',
'Epic', 'The Great Hunger', 'The Hospital', 'In Memory of
my Mother', 'Inniskeen Road: July Evening', 'Innocence',
'Kerr's Ass', 'The Long Garden', 'Memory of Brother
Michael', 'Memory of my Father', 'Peace', 'Pegasus',
'Prelude', 'Pursuit of an Ideal', 'Shancoduff', 'Spraying the
Potatoes', an excerpt from 'Tarry Flynn', 'Temptation in
Harvest', 'To the Man after the Harrow' from *Collected
Poems* (1972) by Patrick Kavanagh; Dolmen Press for
'Ancestor', 'Another September', 'Baggot Street Deserta',
'Ballydavid Pier', 'Downstream', 'In the Ringwood',
'Leaf-Eater', 'Love', 'Mirror in February', 'Song',
'Touching the River', 'Wormwood' from *Poems 1956–1973*
by Thomas Kinsella; Dolmen Press for 'His Father's
Hands', 'Tao and Unfitness at Inistiogue on the River
Nore' from *Peppercanister Poems 1972–1978* by Thomas
Kinsella; The Salamander Press Ltd for 'Caravan',
'Fleance', 'In Memoriam', 'Leaving Inishmore', 'Letter to
Derek Mahon', 'Letter to Seamus Heaney', 'The Linen
Workers', 'The Lodger', 'Man Lying on a Wall', 'No
Continuing City', 'Persephone', 'Second Sight', 'Skara
Brae', 'Swans Mating', 'The Third Light', 'Wounds' from
Poems 1963–1983 (1985) by Michael Longley; Faber & Faber
Ltd for 'Autobiography', an excerpt from 'Autumn Journal',
an excerpt from 'Autumn Sequel', 'Bad Dream', 'The
Blasphemies', 'The Brandy Glass', 'Carrickfergus',
'Charon', 'Coda', 'Cushendun' from 'The Closing Album'
'Eclogue between the Motherless', 'Elegy for Minor Poets',
'Epitaph for Liberal Poets', 'Flight of the Heart', an excerpt

ACKNOWLEDGEMENTS

from 'A Hand of Snapshots' ('The Left-Behind', 'The Once-in-Passing'), an excerpt from 'Nature Notes' ('Dandelions', 'Cats', 'Corncrakes', 'The Sea'), 'Hold-up', 'The Introduction', 'Meeting Point', 'Novelettes III: *The Gardener*', 'Prayer before Birth', 'Reflections', 'River in Spate', 'Slow Movement', 'Snow', 'Soap Suds', 'The Suicide', 'Sunday Morning', 'The Taxis', 'Train to Dublin', 'Tree Party', 'The Truisms', 'Under the Mountain', 'Valediction', 'Woods' from *The Collected Poems of Louis MacNeice* (1966); Oxford University Press for 'Autobiographies', 'A Disused Shed in Co. Wexford', 'Father-in-Law', 'Glengormley', 'Grandfather', 'Homage to Malcolm Lowry', 'In Carrowdore Churchyard', 'The Last of the Fire Kings', 'Lives', 'The Mute Phenomena', 'My Wicked Uncle', 'Nostalgias', 'Poem Beginning with a Line by Cavafy', 'The Poets of the Nineties', 'The Snow Party', 'The Spring Vacation', 'The Studio', 'An Unborn Child' from *Poems 1962–1978* by Derek Mahon © Derek Mahon 1979, reprinted by permission of Oxford University Press; Oxford University Press for 'Courtyards in Delft', 'A Garage in Co. Cork', 'A Lighthouse in Maine', 'Tractatus' from *The Hunt by Night* by Derek Mahon © Derek Mahon 1982, reprinted by permission of Oxford University Press; Interim Press for 'The Cure', 'Gateposts', 'June', 'Smoke', 'Tobacco Hole' from *Single Ladies* by Medbh McGuckian; Oxford University Press for 'The Aphrodisiac', 'Champagne', 'The Flitting', 'The Flower Master', 'The Moon Pond', 'Mr McGregor's Garden', 'Power-Cut', 'The Seed-Picture', 'Slips', 'The Sofa', 'The Standing', 'To my Grandmother', 'Tulips' from *The Flower Master* by Medbh McGuckian © Medbh McGuckian 1982, reprinted by permission of Oxford University Press; Oxford University Press for 'Aviary',

[413]

ACKNOWLEDGEMENTS

'Felicia's Café', 'The Hard Summer', 'On not being your Lover', 'Venus and the Rain' from *Venus and the Rain* by Medbh McGuckian © Medbh McGuckian 1984, reprinted by permission of Oxford University Press; Dolmen Press and Harold Matson Company, Inc. for 'All Legendary Obstacles', 'A Bright Day', 'The Cage', 'Clear the Way', 'Coming Events', 'The Country Fiddler', 'A Drink of Milk', '11 rue Daguerre', 'Herbert Street Revisited', 'Last Journey', 'Mad Sweeny', 'Like Dolmens round my Childhood, the Old People', 'Penal Rock: Altamuskin', 'Return', 'The Road's End', 'Soliloquy on a Southern Strand', 'Sunset', 'Tim', 'Tracks', 'The Trout', 'The Water Carrier', 'A Welcoming Party', 'Windharp' from *Selected Poems* by John Montague © 1982 by John Montague, reprinted by permission of Harold Matson Company, Inc. and the author; Dolmen Press and Harold Matson Company, Inc. for 'The Silver Flask' from *The Dead Kingdom* by John Montague © 1984 by John Montague, reprinted by permission of Harold Matson Company, Inc. and the author; Faber and Faber Ltd for 'Arthur', 'Ballywaire', 'Cadaver Politic', 'From', 'The Hyperboreans', 'Inishkeel Parish Church', 'Newness', 'Settlers', 'States', 'Thinking of Iceland' from *A State of Justice* (1977) by Tom Paulin; Faber & Faber Ltd for 'Anastasia McLaughlin', 'The Other Voice', 'Personal Column', 'Song for February', 'Still Century', 'Where Art is a Midwife' from *The Strange Museum* (1980) by Tom Paulin; Faber & Faber Ltd for 'And Where Do You Stand on the National Question?', 'The Book of Juniper', 'Descendancy', 'Desertmartin', 'Manichean Geography I', 'Of Difference Does it Make', 'Off the Back of a Lorry', 'Politik', 'A Rum Cove, a Stout Cove', 'A Written Answer' from *Liberty Tree* (1983) by Tom Paulin.